The Antietam Paintings by James Hope

Bradley M. Gottfried & Linda I. Gottfried

Turning Point Press
Fayetteville, Pennsylvania

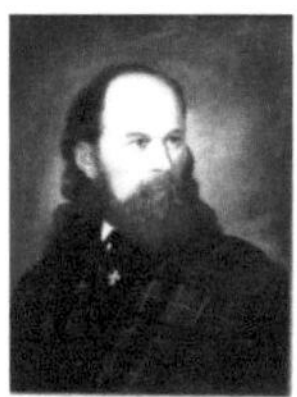

Copyright 2022 by Bradley M. Gottfried & Linda I. Gottfried

Library of Congress Control Number: 2022908969

Designed by Linda I. Gottfried
Set in Garamond

ISBN: 979-8-218-0141107

Published by Turning Point Press

Front Cover: *Artillery Hell* and A *Fateful Turn* by James Hope

Rear Cover: *A Crucial Delay, Wasted Gallantry, The Aftermath at Bloody Lane*

Table of Contents

Introduction to the Hope Paintings

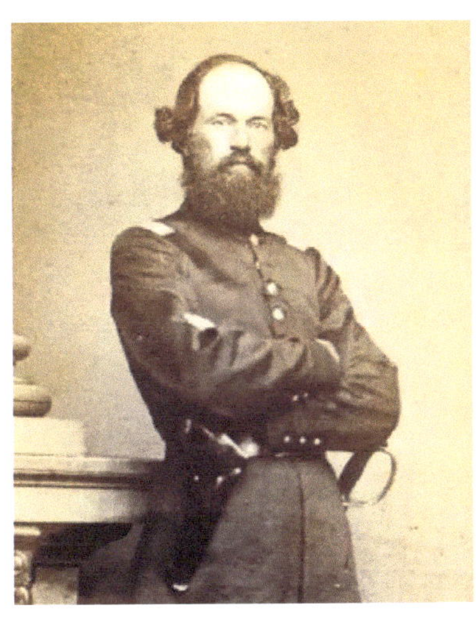

Capt. James Hope
(NPS/Antietam National Battlefield)

James Hope was born in Drygrange, Scotland (the Southern Uplands) on November 29, 1819. His earliest recollections were those of "the exquisite scenery and lordly tales of my Scottish homeland [that] sparked a lifelong attachment for reverent delight in Nation so Attuned, with Fervent Love for right and valor so Nurtured." His mother died before he turned two years old and he moved to Canada with his father when he was nine. His father died a few years later, leaving the 16-year-old homeless and penniless, so he decided to seek his fortune in the United States.

Hope walked 150 miles to Fairhaven, Vermont, where he apprenticed for five years with a local wagon maker. He saved enough money to take an art course at the Castleton Vermont Seminary/Academy (now Castleton State College). This led to a bout of teaching art in West Rutland, Vermont. He married Julia Smith of Rutland on September 20, 1842, forcing him to earn a living as a full-time teacher at the cost of his artistic pursuits. This changed when he sustained a serious leg wound while chopping wood. During a long recuperation, he again took up the paint brush and created a self-portrait. Word of his proficiency quickly spread and he received a number of commissions, some paying as much as $100. While Hope was a talented portraitist, his passion was in painting landscapes and he decided to charge high prices to sustain his interest in landscape painting "for which there was no ready market but which possessed my soul," he later wrote. Hope realized he needed to relocate to a larger community in order to maximize his profits, so he moved his family (wife and two children at the time) to Montreal, Canada in 1848. He found success in these endeavors, but two years after moving, realized the cold weather was taking its toll on his family, so he moved them back to Castleton, Vermont, where he built a house and taught drawing and painting at the nearby Academy. His family would grow to six with the addition of two children during this period.

Hope was mentored there by some established artists as he perfected his landscape techniques. However, he realized he needed to again move to a larger city to earn a suitable living, so he opened a studio on 5th Avenue in New York City in 1852. He began splitting his time, spending winters in New York and summers in Vermont.

With the outbreak of the Civil War, 43-year-old Hope assisted in recruiting Company B of the 2nd Vermont Infantry, which mustered into Federal service on June 1, 1861. Hope became a captain in the regiment, and saw action at First Bull Run and subsequent battles, including Antietam. Hope had a stint as a topographical engineer, which gave him the luxury of sketching various terrain features. He retained a sketchbook to record observations with the intention they would become "huge historical panoramas to preserve for posterity." His health deteriorated while in the army. He first contracted malaria and then dysentery. Rheumatism of the knees added to Hope's misery, forcing him to resign his commission and leave the army on December 20, 1862.

Upon returning home, Hope immediately began creating military-related canvases based on his sketches and personal recollections. Immediately after the war, he helped illustrate a book on the personal recollections of army surgeon George Stevens. During this time, Hope

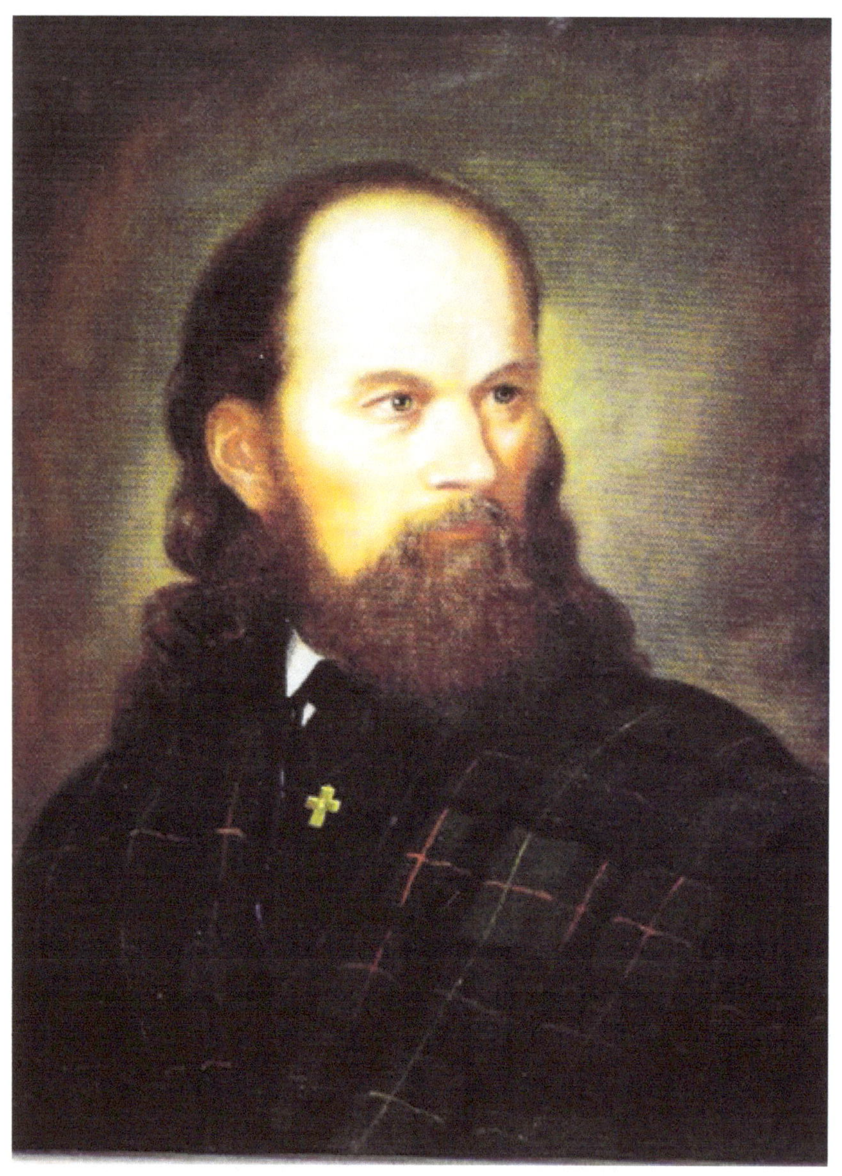

1865 Oil on canvas
Self portrait

stumbled upon Watkins Glen and was taken by its beauty, which reminded him of his native Scotland. He sold his properties in New York City and Vermont and moved his family into a Swiss Chalet built high up in the Glen. He hoped his savings and future commissions "from the fashionables watering at the Spa" would provide all that was necessary to live a comfortable life. Hope established a gallery containing 84 of his paintings and made available to the viewing public for a fee.

James Hope was a prominent member of the Hudson River School of 19th century landscapists that included Thomas Cole, George Inness and Jasper Cropsey. In addition to his famed landscapes, Hope felt honor-bound to record the events of the American Civil War. He embarked on a series of small canvases (18 by 26 inches) covering First and Second Bull Run, the Peninsula Campaign, Fredericksburg, Gettysburg, and Antietam. He also endeavored to translate these smaller works into panoramic canvases.

After attending two reunions during the late 1880's, Hope made additional Antietam sketches and completed older ones. He completed the five large Antietam panoramas (5.5ft. by 12ft.) in time for the 30th anniversary of the battle, which were displayed in Washington, D.C. Hope's works were well-received by the veterans, although one complained there should have been more bodies lying in the fields. The last twenty years of his life (1872-1892) were probably his most prolific as he churned out canvas after canvas. During the last years of his life he continued attending church services and wrote poetry. He died on October 20, 1892, and was buried in the cemetery behind his house.

Hope bequeathed his artwork to his only son, who became a talented photographer, and kept his father's studio open for visitors to admire his father's works. When Hope's son died, the property went to his two children. The paintings suffered a near death experience when the studio was all but destroyed by a flood in 1935. All but one of the paintings were rescued in fairly good condition and sold to a private collector. The exception was The Aftermath at Bloody Lane canvas discovered under a ton of silt from the flood that had occurred 20 years before and was destroyed beyond recovery, except for a small section.

The remaining Antietam panoramas were hung in the eaves of a church, where they were further damaged by birds and rodents. The National Park Service purchased the paintings in 1979 for $5,000 and immediately removed them. The process was difficult, as they were nailed to the wall with six-inch spikes. The large paintings each weigh more than 200 pounds, making their removal even more difficult. They were then sent out to be restored at a cost of more than $10,000 apiece. A second restoration occurred in 2021-22 when the old Antietam National Battlefield Visitors Center was closed for renovations.

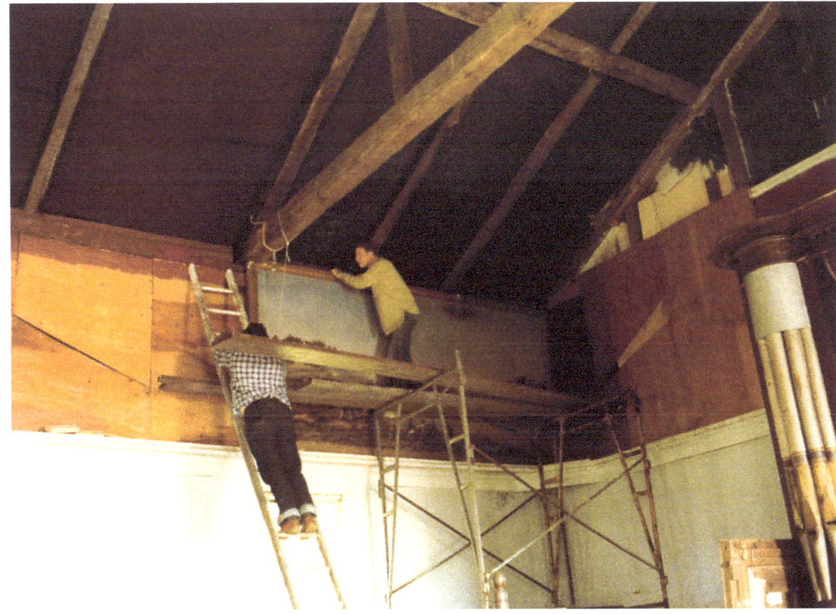
Removing the Hope paintings
Courtesy of NPS/Antietam National Battlefield

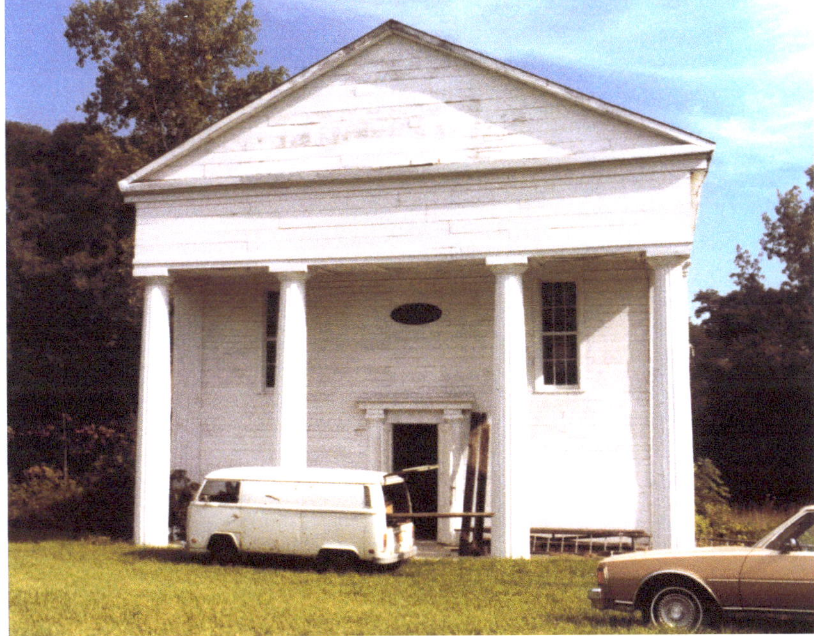
Church where the Antietam Paintings were stored
Courtesy of NPS/Antietam National Battlefield

While known for their vivid portrayal of several actions at Antietam, one must exercise caution when attempting to interpret them, as Hope often crammed several hours of combat into each painting. For example, "Artillery Hell" probably includes action from 7:30 a.m. through 10:00 a.m. Nevertheless, they depict in vivid detail, important events in the battle and are truly a treasure.

The Hope Antietam paintings will continue to be available to the general public, but only one will be on display at a time to better ensure the preservation of these treasures. With that knowledge, we prepared this book to help ensure that all can enjoy the paintings even if they are not on display. Linda and I also wanted to show the detailed nature of these paintings by enlarging sections of the five panoramas.

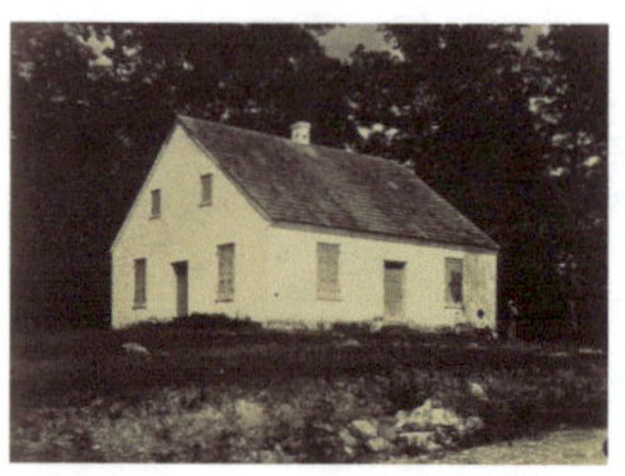

Dunker Church before the battle
(Library of Congress)

This panorama represents the action along Hagerstown Pike, looking northwest. It is actually a continuation of the battle to the left (west) of the battle scene represented in the "A Fateful Turn" canvas. The painting is expansive; illustrating the action between 7:00 a.m. and 10:00 a.m. Col. Stephen Lee's Confederate artillery battalion dominates the foreground, firing at Union troops attempting to capture the Miller Cornfield (in the distance), although in Hope's depiction, some of the cannon appear to be firing to the south. The scene shifts to a later time, about 8:45 a.m., when Maj. Gen. John Sedgwick's division (in three lines) is making its way toward the West Woods. Although not illustrated, the division entered the West Woods, only to be attacked from multiple directions by Maj. Gen. Lafayette McLaws' Confederate division, which had just reached the battlefield after an all-night march from Harpers Ferry. An earlier attack of the XII Corps had already driven Stephen Lee's artillery from its high-ground positions by the time of Sedgwick's attack. Other major features of this painting include the Dunker Church, the West and East Woods and the Miller Cornfield (in the distance) where intense fighting occurred.

Artillery Hell Looking West

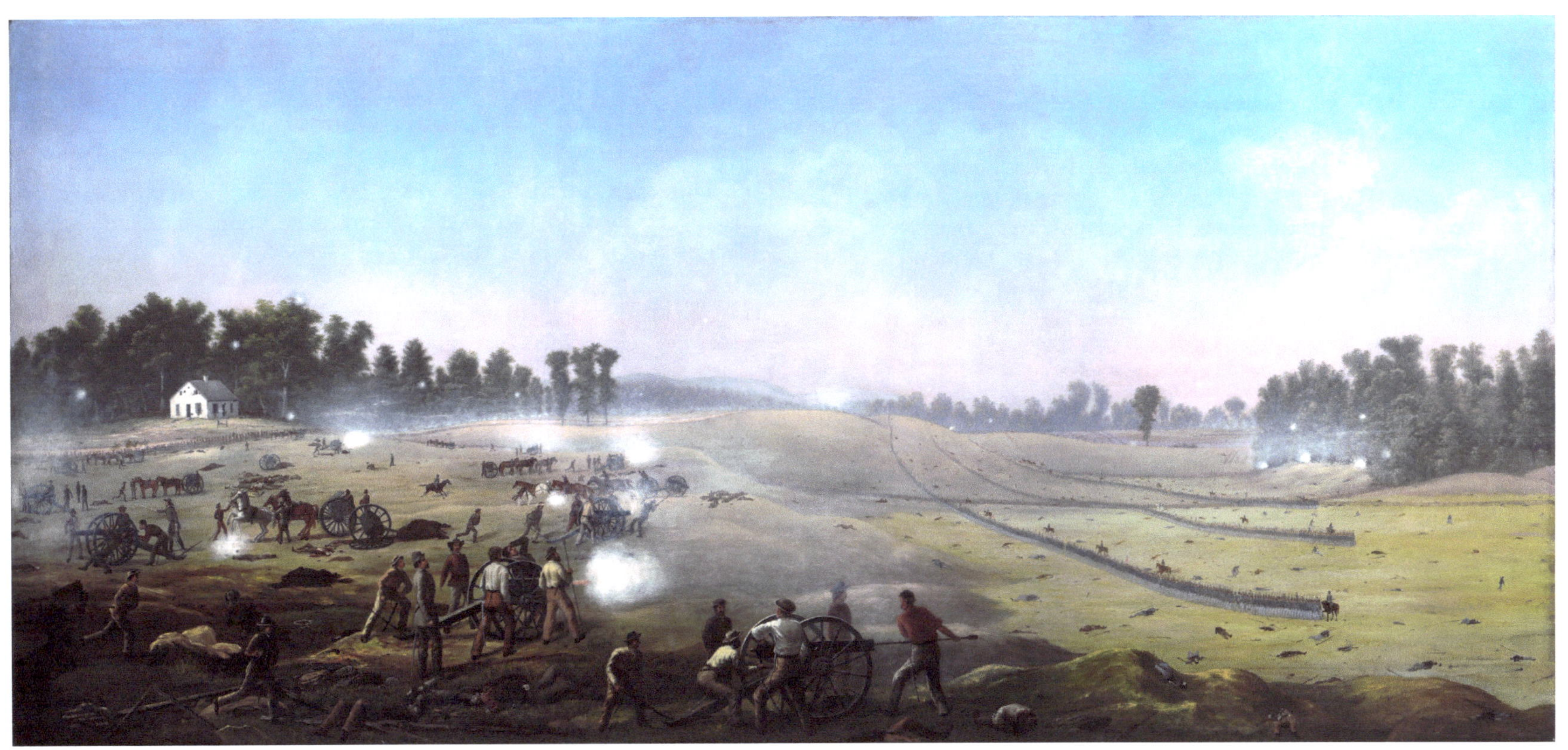

James Hope, Artillery Hell, Oil on Canvas
Courtesy of NPS/Antietam National Battlefield

A. Confederate artillery battery in action: It is unclear who these cannon are engaging as they are facing south, toward Sharpsburg, held by the Confederates. Each cannon was served by a crew of eight men.

B. Limber: These wheeled vehicles contained an ammunition chest and a hook attached to the rear to move the cannon. Three members of the cannon's crew were stationed at the limbers: the two cannoneers who cut the fuses so the shells would burst at the appropriate time and the runner who brought the shell to the cannon crew. Because of the volatility of the ammunition within the limber chests, they were usually kept several yards in the rear of the battery. Not shown are the caissons, which contained two additional ammunition chests and remained even further to the rear for their protection.

C. Dead cannoneers and disabled limber: James Hope clearly used the photograph taken by Alexander Gardner a few days after the battle as a model for his painting of the disabled limber and dead cannoneers (see lower right of this page).

D. Horses: Horses were an invaluable resource for both armies. They not only pulled the wagons and artillery, they carried officers and aides. It was not unusual for a cannon or limber to be lost/abandoned because of the death of the horses needed to pull them to safety. These animals had to remain calm under intense cannon fire, but when a shell exploded nearby, they were prone to panic, as can be seen here.

E. Hagerstown Pike: This turnpike was one of the reasons Lee selected this battleground, as it ran directly to Hagerstown and then into Pennsylvania. Because it was paved with macadam, travelers were able to make their way to their destination without the typical ruts and mud of traditional dirt roads. Like today's turnpikes, they carried a toll to use them.

F. Confederate troops along Hagerstown Pike: The identity of these infantry is unclear, but could be Confederates from Brig. Gen. Joseph Kershaw's brigade or Col. Van Manning's brigade. Both charged out of the West Woods after the XII Corps had driven Stephen Lee's guns from their positions near the Dunker Church and after Sedgwick's division was defeated in the West Woods.

G. Dunker Church: Built in 1852 by a congregation of the German Baptist Brethren, it sustained major damage during the battle and is depicted in Gardner's photograph (see below).

H. West Woods: At the beginning of the battle, these woods hid thousands of Confederate reinforcements, and later, intense fighting occurred here.

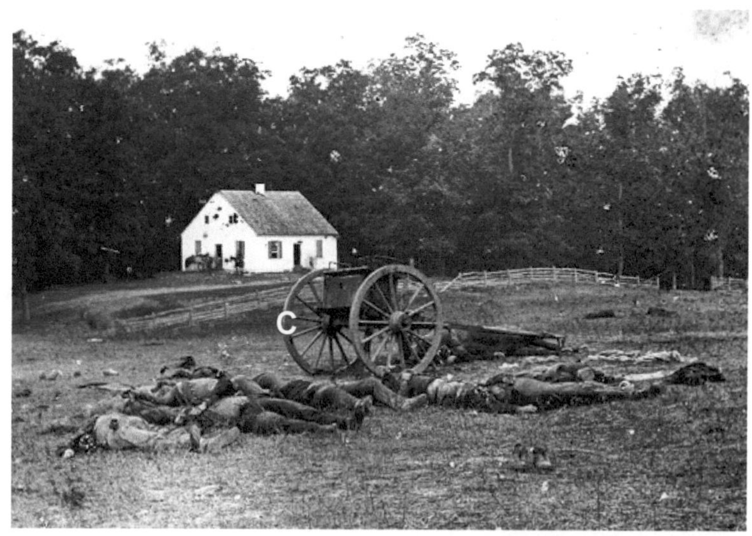

Alexander Garner photograph
(Library of Congress)

Artillery Hell Left Side of Painting

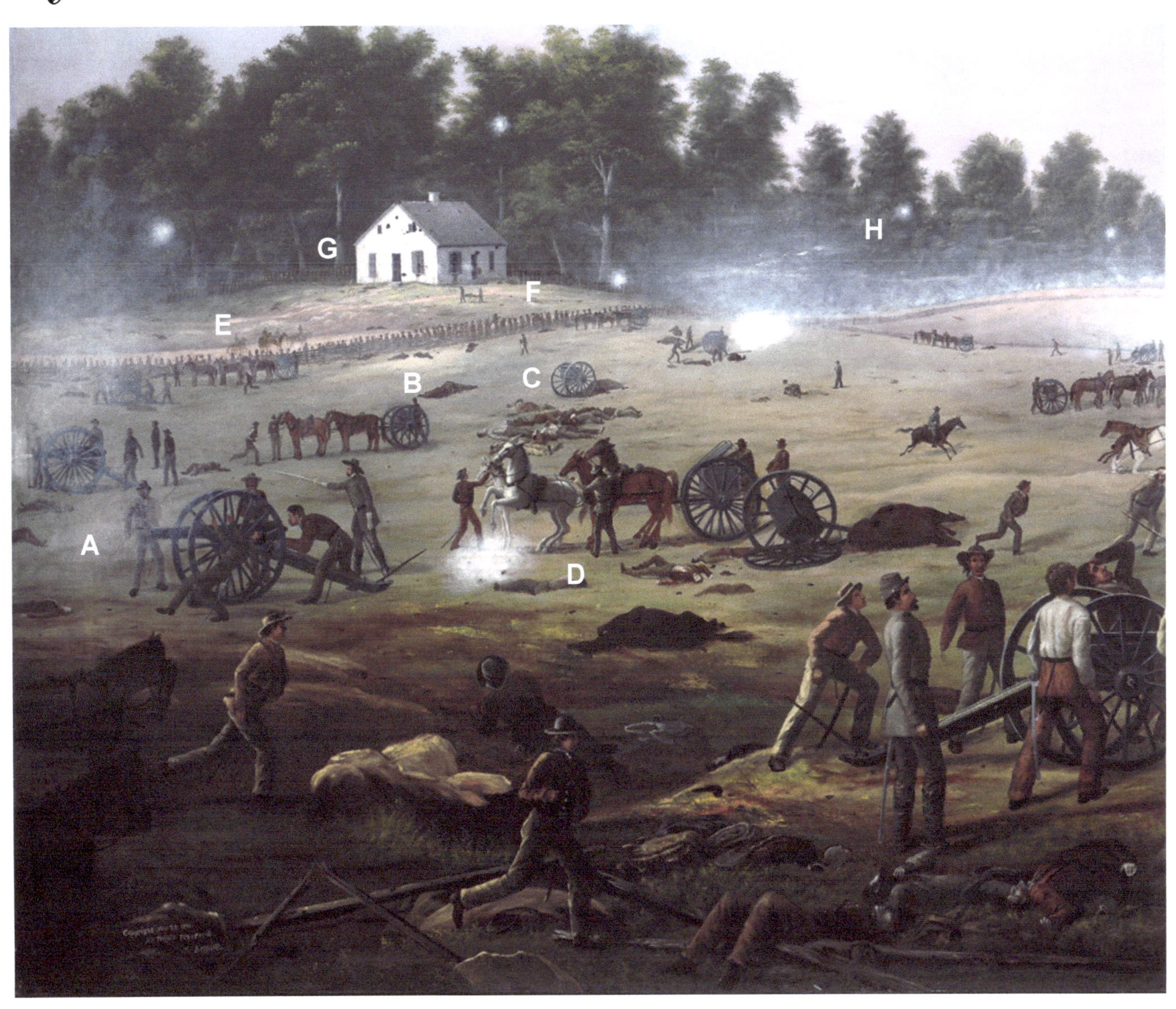

A. Confederate artillery crew in action: These cannon were part of Stephen Lee's Artillery Battalion and were firing north at Union troops attempting to capture the Miller Cornfield. The cannon crew in the foreground illustrates how Civil War cannons were fired. Six surround the cannon. They included #1 (right front), who sponges down the barrel after firing and handles the rammer to push the shell down into the tube; #2 (left front), who handles the "worm"—a long rod that removed burning debris accumulated in the barrel after a cannon is fired and also loads the piece; #3 (right rear) puts his thumb on the vent on top of the cannon so air does not enter, while #1 rams the round into the barrel, preventing premature ignition. He also punctures the powder bag at the base of the projectile; #4 (left rear), inserts the friction primer and fires the guns with the lanyard. A sixth man (to the rear of the cannon) is seen with a hand spike, moving the gun from right to left as the gunner aims it, although his main duty is probably crew position #3, #5 carries the shell from the limber to the cannon. The Gunner (crouched down directly behind the barrel) commands the gun is shown sighting it. Two others were needed, but are back at the limber preparing shells for firing.

B. Cannon firing: When a cannon fired, the #1 and #2 usually held their ears, lest they become deafened from the explosion.

C. Cannoneers under fire: Opposing artillery tried to neutralize the enemy's cannon, so being a cannoneer was a hazardous occupation. Bodies of dead cannoneers can be seen as a shell bursts near a #1 cannoneer, probably putting him out of action.

D. Cannon attached to limber and heading for the rear: It was not unusual for cannon to be moved during a battle, usually to be repositioned or to avoid intense enemy counter-battery fire. This cannon appears to be moving to the rear because all of its cannoneers are lying on the ground and out of action.

E. Hagerstown Pike: The turnpike was lined by sturdy post and rail fences. Infantry from both armies moved from one side of the pike to the others to attack the enemy at some points in the battle. During the earliest part of the battle, part of Doubleday's division used it to approach Lee's left flank held by Maj. Gen. Thomas "Stonewall" Jackson's men.

F. North Woods: No fighting occurred in the North Woods, at the far reaches of the battlefield. However, the Union I Corps under Maj. Gen. Joseph Hooker occupied this general area the evening before the battle, and it was the jumping off point for the earliest attacks on Miller's Cornfield.

G. West Woods: Like the East Woods, the West Woods saw intense fighting during the morning and midday hours of the battle and was controlled by both sides at various times.

H. Campbell's/Stewart's battery: According to Hope, the smoke in the distance is from Capt. James Campbell's battery, in action along Hagerstown Pike.

I. David Miller House: Hope added the Miller house to this portion of the painting. The bloody cornfield belonged to Miller. For the major destruction of his crops, loss of livestock, and personal belongings, Miller received the equivalent of about $25,000 in compensation from the government.

Artillery Hell Middle of Painting

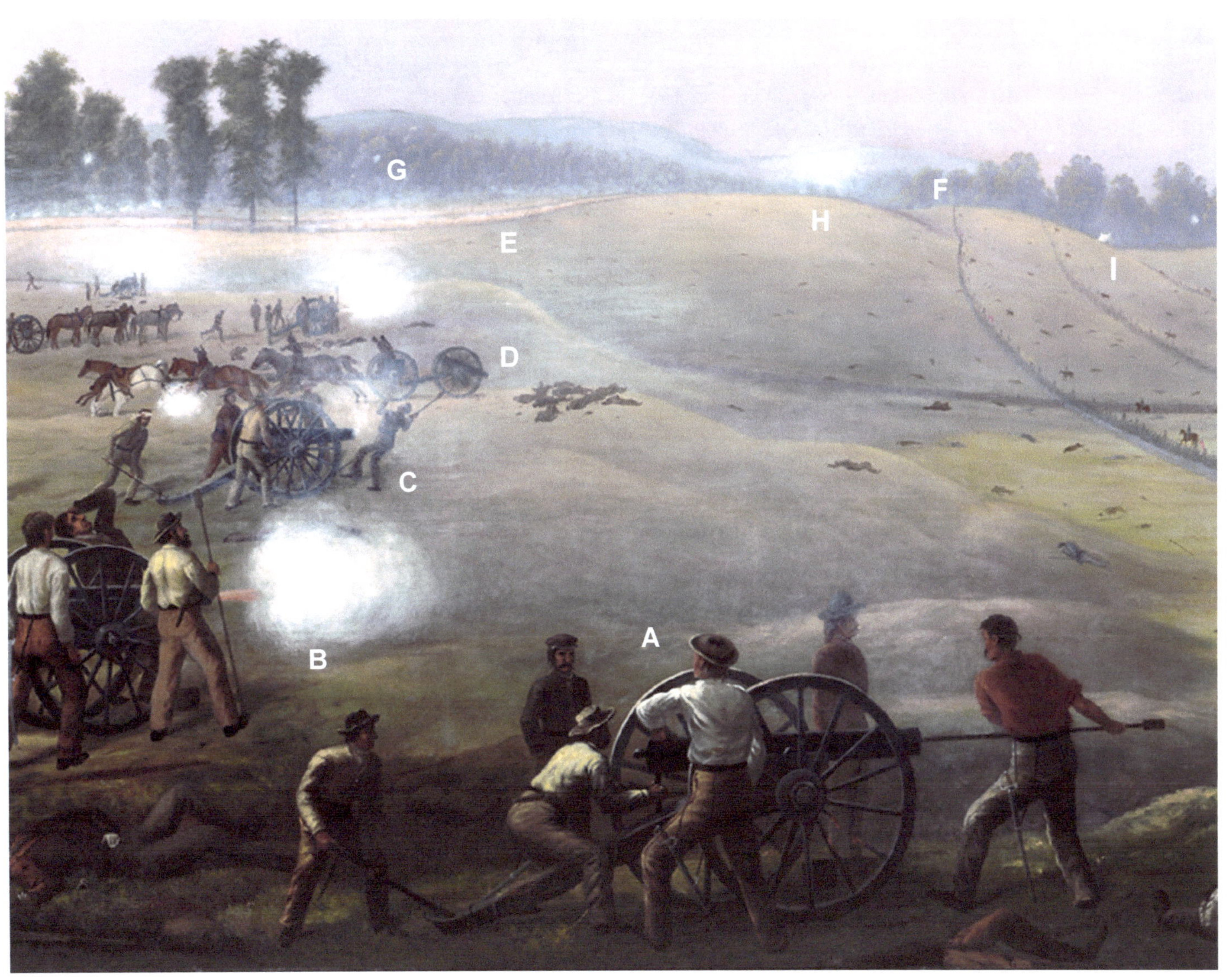

A. Sedgwick's division: The right side of the painting is dominated by the impressive charge of Maj. Gen. John Sedgwick's Union division (II Corps) at about 9:15 a.m. The Miller Cornfield was already in Union hands when this large, 5,500-man division emerged from the East Woods **(B)** and headed across the open fields to the West Woods to clear out the remainder of the Confederates who still occupied it. The division was organized into three brigades, who advanced in that fashion. Brig. Gen. Willis Gorman's brigade formed the first line; Brig. Gen. Napoleon Dana's the second line; Brig. Gen. Oliver Howard's Philadelphia Brigade was in the rear. The division initially received orders to cross Antietam Creek at about 7:20 a.m. and quickly marched to the battlefield.

C. Infantry advance: The letter is next to a regiment's flag, which can barely be seen in this painting. Because of the intense white smoke and ear-splitting noise of battle, infantry units advanced shoulder-to-shoulder to maintain cohesion. The flag was used to help direct the movement of the regiment under these intense situations. Usually, only the three field officers were mounted: on one end of the regiment rode the lieutenant colonel, the major was found at the opposite end, and the colonel who commanded the regiment, rode behind the flag, yelling out orders to be obeyed by the flag bearer.

D. Killed and wounded troops: Troops advancing over open areas were usually pounded by enemy artillery. The dead and wounded from prior fighting and during the advance can be seen dotting the field.

E. Wounded soldier heading for the rear: Those men who were wounded made their way to the rear, if they were able. This better assured their survival as they could receive immediate medical attention, compared to those who were immobile and forced to wait until the hostilities ended.

F. Miller Cornfield: The Cornfield was the site of intense fighting during the early phase of the battle. It appears fairly sterile in this part of the painting, but in reality, thousands of dead and wounded littered the field.

G. East Woods/cannon: The East Woods saw extensive fighting during the battle of Antietam. The night before the battle, these woods hosted the 13th Pennsylvania Reserves which skirmished with Confederates under Brig. Gen. John Hood until nightfall. The East Woods also experienced fighting through 8:30 a.m. on the morning of the battle. By the time Sedgwick made his attack on the West Woods, these woods were finally under Union control. The artillery shown here firing from the edge of the woods **(H)** were probably batteries from the Union XII Corps, lined up axle to axle. This forced them to fire over the heads of their own infantry, and sometimes shells fell among them, causing their outrage.

I. Smoketown Road: This road was an important thoroughfare for moving Union troops toward the battlefield and intense fighting also occurred along some parts of it, particularly near the East Woods.

J. Union troops reforming: These troops are probably elements of the I and XII Corps who fought for several hours to secure the Miller Cornfield and East Woods.

Artillery Hell Right Side of Painting

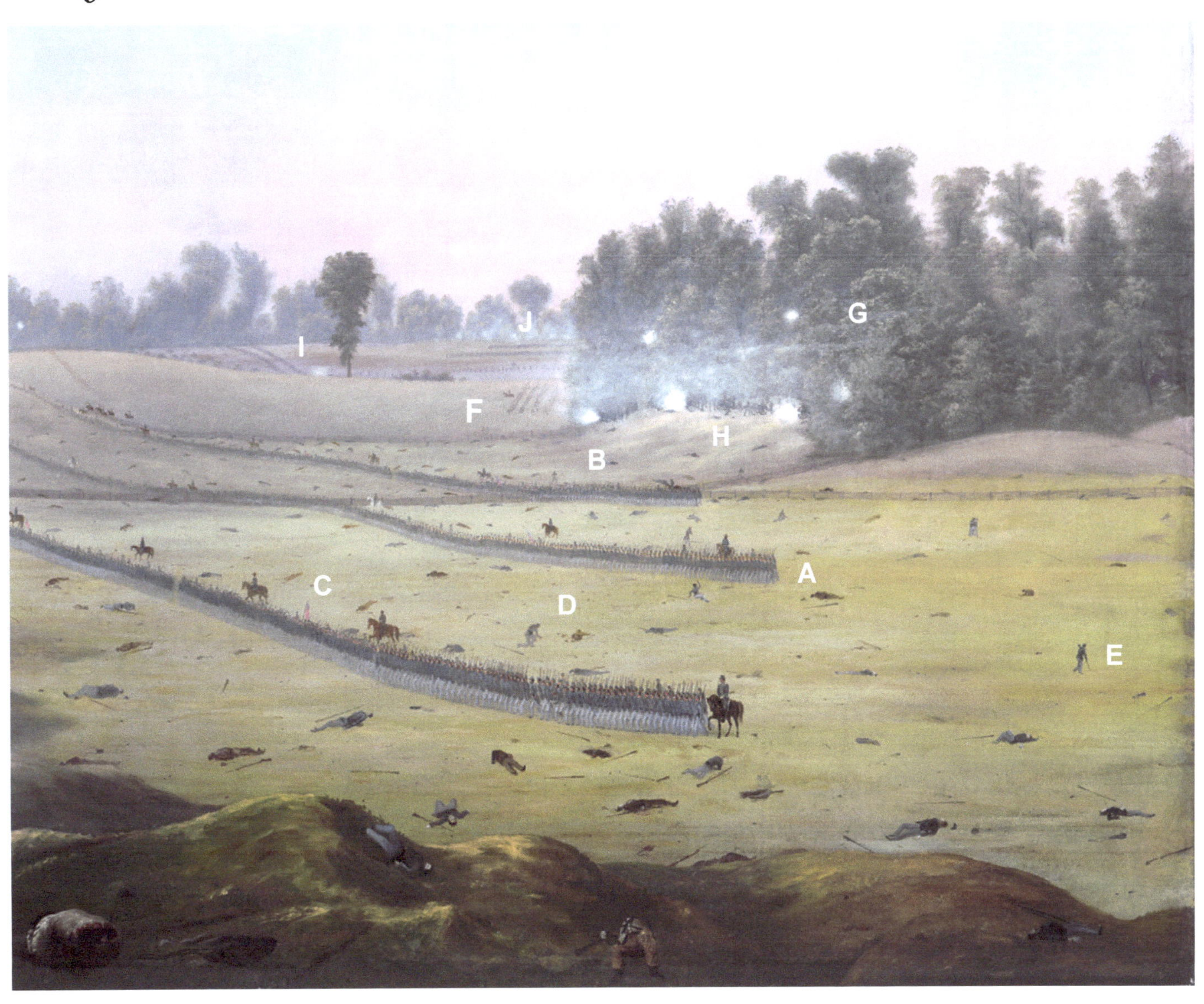

This canvas represents events to the east of the "Artillery Hell" painting, and captures the area between the East Woods and the Sunken Road between 11:00 a.m. and 2:00 p.m. After the fighting died down in the Miller Cornfield around 8:30 a.m., the fight shifted to the West Woods where Sedgwick's division was decimated by McLaws' Confederate division, losing about 40% of its men in 20 minutes (see "Artillery Hell"). The fight for the Sunken Road is illustrated on the right side of the canvas, with long lines of the Union II Corps attacking several thousand Confederate defenders in what would become known as the Bloody Lane. The latter was actually part of the Sunken Road, which was used as a shortcut by farmers and extended from Hagerstown Pike to Boonsboro Pike, initially provided a good defensive position. The two Union divisions that fought for possession of the Bloody Lane, Brig. Gen. William French's and Maj. Gen. Israel Richardson's, had earlier splashed across Antietam Creek below the Upper Bridge and headed south. Upon reaching the area around the Roulette house, the units made "A Fateful Turn" toward the Sunken Road. Fighting began at 9:15 a.m., with French's division initially attacking the Bloody Lane. The Union divisions were finally successful in driving the Confederates from the Sunken Road at about noon.

Fighting then continued in the Piper farm fields (see "Wasted Gallantry") as Richardson's men attempted to reach the town of Sharpsburg, which would drive a wedge in the center of the Confederate army and cut off its retreat route to the Potomac River at Shepherdstown. Several homes can be seen in this depiction, including the Mumma farm (set on fire by the Confederates), the Roulette farm in the center of the frame, and in the distance, the Pry house (McClellan's headquarters for part of the battle). The heights of South Mountain and Elk Ridge are prominent in this representation. Unlike the five other works, Hope has the viewer hovering over the battlefield for a "bird's-eye" view of the action.

A Fateful Turn Looking North

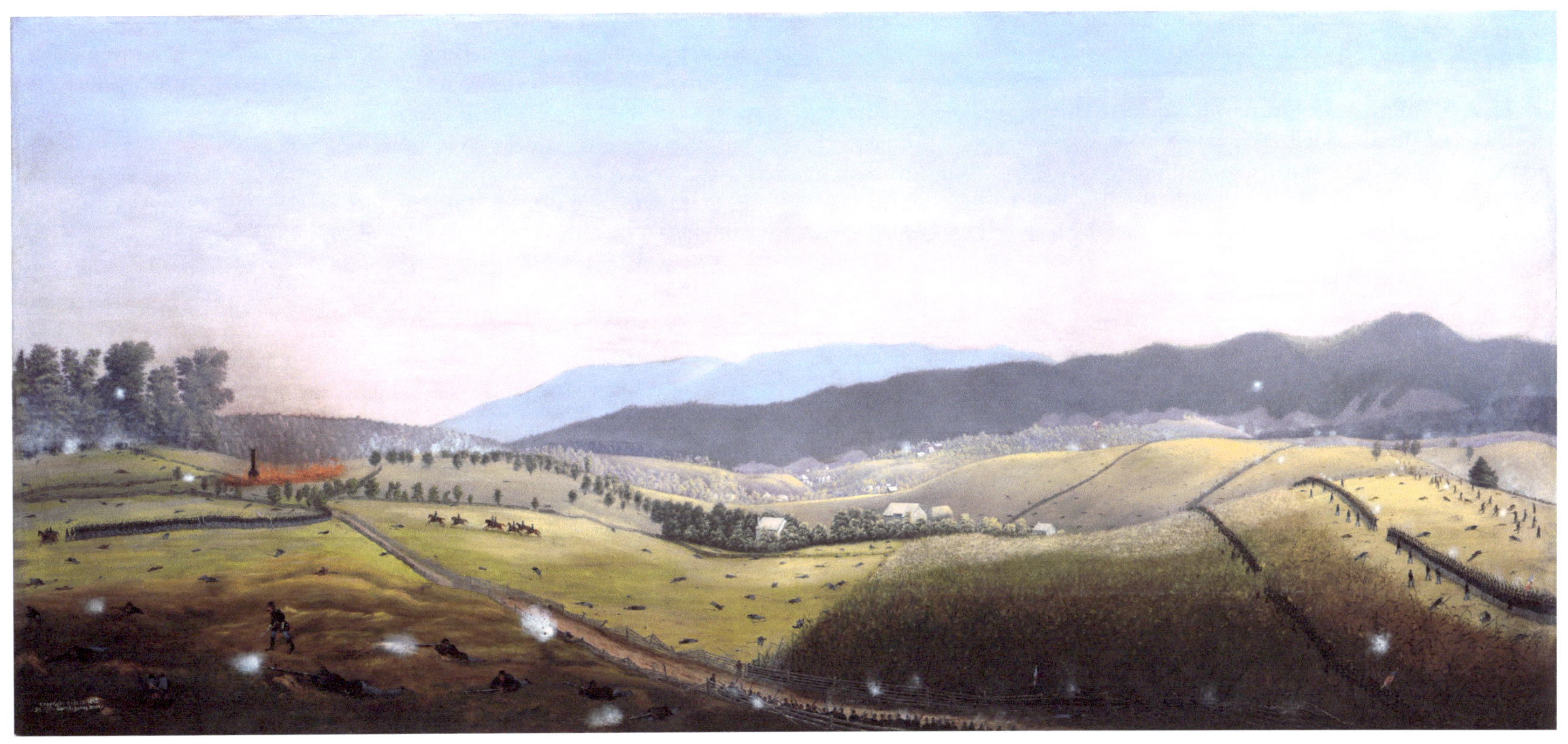

James Hope, *A Fateful Turn,* Oil on Canvas
Courtesy of NPS/Antietam National Battlefield

A. Union batteries in front of East Woods: Several Union batteries were in action in front of the East Woods shelling Confederate formations near the West Woods. These probably included Lt. George Woodruff's and Capt. George Cothran's batteries.

B. Union infantry column: The identity of this infantry column is unclear, but they are definitely marching toward the West Woods, led by their officers. The most logical unit would be Col. William Irwin's brigade (Maj. Gen. William Smith's division, VI Corps), which was rushed toward the west to blunt a determined attack by two Confederate regiments (3rd Arkansas and 27th North Carolina of Manning's Brigade) on Brig. Gen. William French's division's right flank.

C. Mumma farm ablaze (see artist's representation in the narrative for the right side of the painting: During the early morning of the battle, Brig. Gen. Roswell Ripley, whose Confederate brigade occupied the area around the Mumma farm buildings, ordered his men to set them ablaze. He explained in his report, "...a set of farm buildings in our front were set on fire to prevent them being made use of by the enemy." A Union soldier recalled, "Just in front of us a house was burning, and the fire and smoke, flashing of muskets and whizzing of bullets, yells of men ...were perfectly horrible." Wealthy land-owner Samuel Mumma would use his own funds to rebuild his farm buildings the following year after he was denied reparations from the U.S. Government.

D. McClellan and his staff: Union army commander, Maj. Gen. George McClellan, crossed Antietam Creek and rode around the battlefield at about 2:00 p.m. He is shown here riding with his staff, probably to observe the deployment of the Union VI Corps.

E. Direction of the Upper Bridge: Three stone bridges over Antietam Creek played a major role in the battle. We will see the Lower Bridge in Hope's "A Crucial Delay" panorama. Only two Union corps (I and XII) crossed at the Upper Bridge; the II and VI Corps and part of the I Corps crossed at fords south of the Upper Bridge to maneuver into position. The Upper Bridge is not shown in this part of the painting, but its approximate location is indicated.

F. Limestone Ledges: Limestone was the most common type of underlying rock formation. These rocks are not visible, except for large rocks and ledges. They were often used by both armies to protect their men from the bullets zipping around them. In many cases, the rocks jutted out from the ground, but were covered by grass and trees. Union soldiers are using these formations for protection while they blaze away at distant Confederates.

G. Union officer: Casualties were especially heavy among the officers, as they were often exposed to small arms and artillery fire. This portion of the painting shows an exposed official giving orders to his protected men.

H. Soldier reloading: Experienced soldiers faced with reloading while in a prone position, usually rolled onto their backs and filled the muzzles of their muskets with bullets and powder mixed together in a cartridge. This figure shows such a soldier in the process of loading his firearm while lying on his back.

I. Wounded Union soldier: Despite the protection, many soldiers were killed and wounded while taking refuge behind these shallow upwellings. This part of the painting clearly shows a soldier who has been wounded.

A Fateful Turn Left Side of Painting

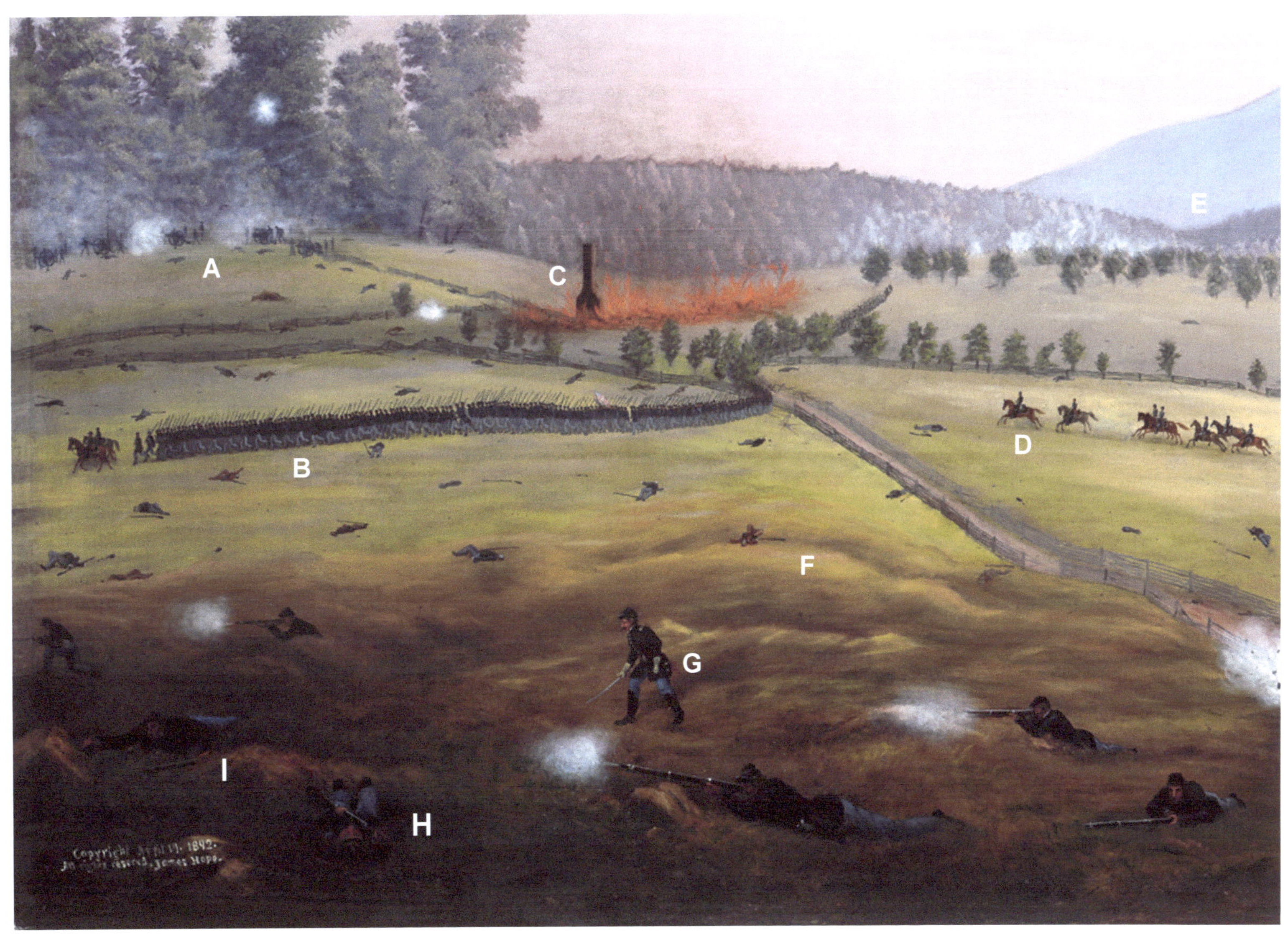

A. Rolling terrain: The battlefield was characterized by a rolling terrain that made troop deployment and command and control difficult. This part of the painting shows the gradually sloping landscape. As one travels south, the terrain is much more rugged (see the "Crucial Delay").

B. South Mountain: Looming over the battlefield, South Mountain is the northern extension of the Blue Ridge Mountains. It runs about 70 miles from the Potomac River in Maryland to Dillsburg, Pennsylvania. It is bisected by several gaps, where roads traverse the mountain. Such a gap is easily visible above the letter "B."

C. Elk Ridge: This ridge sits in front of South Mountain and runs from the Potomac River at Harpers Ferry to Rohrersville, Maryland. The end portion of the Ridge is called "Red Hill" and was the site of a Union signal station that reported on Confederate positions and troop movements, conveying them to a variety of headquarters around the battlefield. These messages were conveyed by signal flags.

D. Pry house: Often mischaracterized as McClellan's headquarters during the entire battle (he was actually riding around the battlefield, spending much time on the east bank of Antietam Creek), the Pry House can be seen in the distance. It is the house with the reddish tinge at the base of Elk Ridge.

E. Roulette house: Mr. William Roulette was perhaps the only civilian who remained on the battlefield during the battle on September 17. As French's division drove past his home, he purportedly ran out of his basement, shouting, "Give it to 'em! Drive 'em!" The house, which was situated in a depression to take advantage of water availability, was struck several times during the battle. Chaplain Henry Stevens of the 14th Connecticut Infantry recalled, "Bullets pierced it on the day of battle, and one huge shell tore through the west side, a little above the floor, and going through the parlor in an upward course passed through the ceiling and a wall beyond…During the battle the rooms were stripped of their furnishings and the floors were covered with the blood and dirt and litter of a field hospital…" Tragedy struck the Roulette family after the battle when their 20-month-old daughter died of disease, probably brought to the area by the soldiers. Mr. Roulette requested $3,500 in reparations from the government to cover the damage to his farm buildings, crops, and livestock, but received only $371 for the hospital portion of his claim.

F. Roulette barn: William Roulette's barn also sustained damage during the battle and also became a field hospital. As the 132nd Pennsylvania, a rookie unit in French's division, marched past the barn on its way to Bloody Lane, a Confederate artillery shell exploded, knocking over the bee hives nearby. The angry bees descended on the Pennsylvanians, causing many to go "rolling in the grass, running, jumping, and ducking." Their commanders saw their plight and ordered the men to "double-quick" past the barn and eventually outpaced the angry bees.

G. Union casualties: The numerous Union casualties were probably caused by intense Confederate artillery fire, which blanketed the area as French's division approached the Bloody Lane.

H. Mumma farm lane: The farm lane was an important thoroughfare for farmers in the area, linking Smoketown Road to the north with the Sunken Road to the south.

I. Destroyed fences: Post and rail fences were prevalent on the battlefield. Known for their durability against the efforts of infantry to knock them down, they were no match against artillery fire, which killed and maimed the infantrymen and knocked over the fences.

A Fateful Turn Middle of Painting

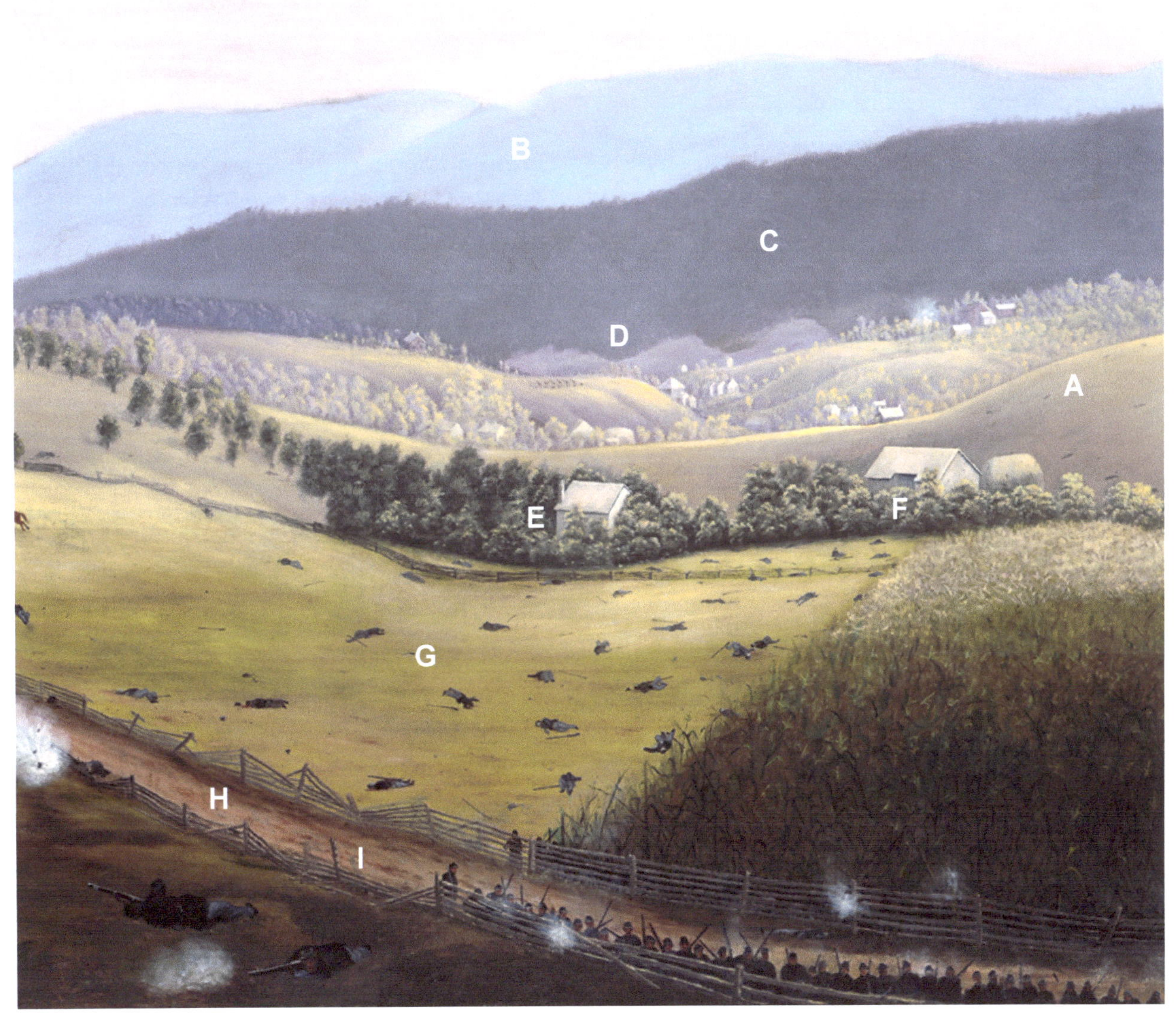

A. Sunken Road/Bloody Lane: The most important part of the "A Fateful Turn," panorama, the Bloody Lane, barely makes it into the frame, being pushed far to the right. Looking closely, you can see Confederates lined up to repulse charge after Union charge.

B. French's division attacking the Bloody Lane: The troops in the foreground are probably from French's division. Numbering over 6,000 men, this division opened the fighting at about 9:15 a.m. Organized into three brigades, each was destined to attack the Bloody Lane sequentially, rather than in tandem. The first two attacks were bloodily repulsed.

C. Troops milling around Bloody Lane: The disordered troops milling around near the Bloody Lane are probably the survivors of Brig. Gen. Max Weber's brigade, the first of French's units to attack the Bloody Lane. This brigade had been pulled from garrison to join French's division and was the first to attempt to drive the Confederates away. They sustained a horrible defeat, losing 582 men in a matter of minutes.

D. French's second line: French's second line was composed of brand-new troops of Col. Dwight Morris' brigade who just learned how to load their weapons. This would be the first time they would fire their weapons and it was in the face of a stout enemy defensive line. This brigade was defeated, losing 529 men.

E. French's third line: French's last line was composed of the veterans of Brig. Gen. Nathan Kimball's brigade. Although experienced, they were not able to drive the North Carolinians and Alabamians from the Bloody Lane, and lost 639 men.

F. Richardson's division: Richardson's division is deployed for action in the distance. It would also attack in waves, with the Irish Brigade launching the first attack. Sporting smooth-bore muskets, only effective at a range of less than 75 yards, these troops were forced to close the distance to the Bloody Lane before they could open fire. The result was severe losses to many of the units. For example, the 69th New York lost more than 62% of its men.

G. Clipp house: This small property on the Roulette farm was rented by Hiram Clipp. It was situated along the Roulette Lane, which is not visible.

H. Reinforcements: Capt. Hope suggests this line of troops was from Brig. Gen. W. T. Brooks' brigade (VI Corps), which had recently arrived on the battlefield. Hope's 2nd Vermont would have been in this line.

I. Red Hill: The high point of Elk Ridge, Red Hill loomed over the battlefield, providing an important observation post.

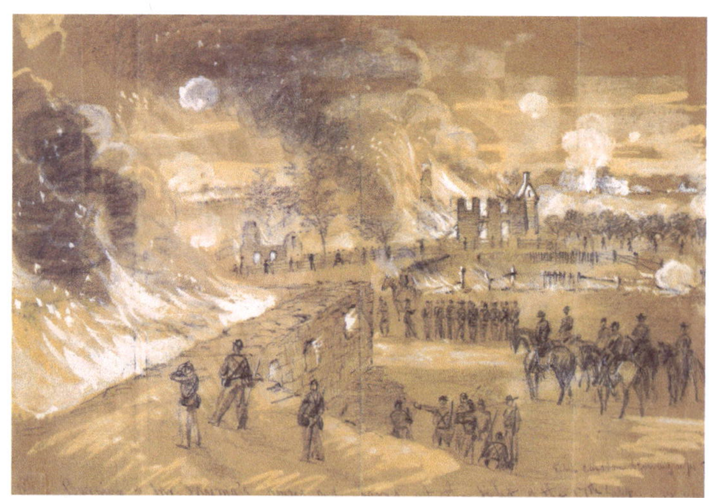

Burning of Mumma Farm by Alfred Waud
(Library of Congress)

A Fateful Turn Right Side of Painting

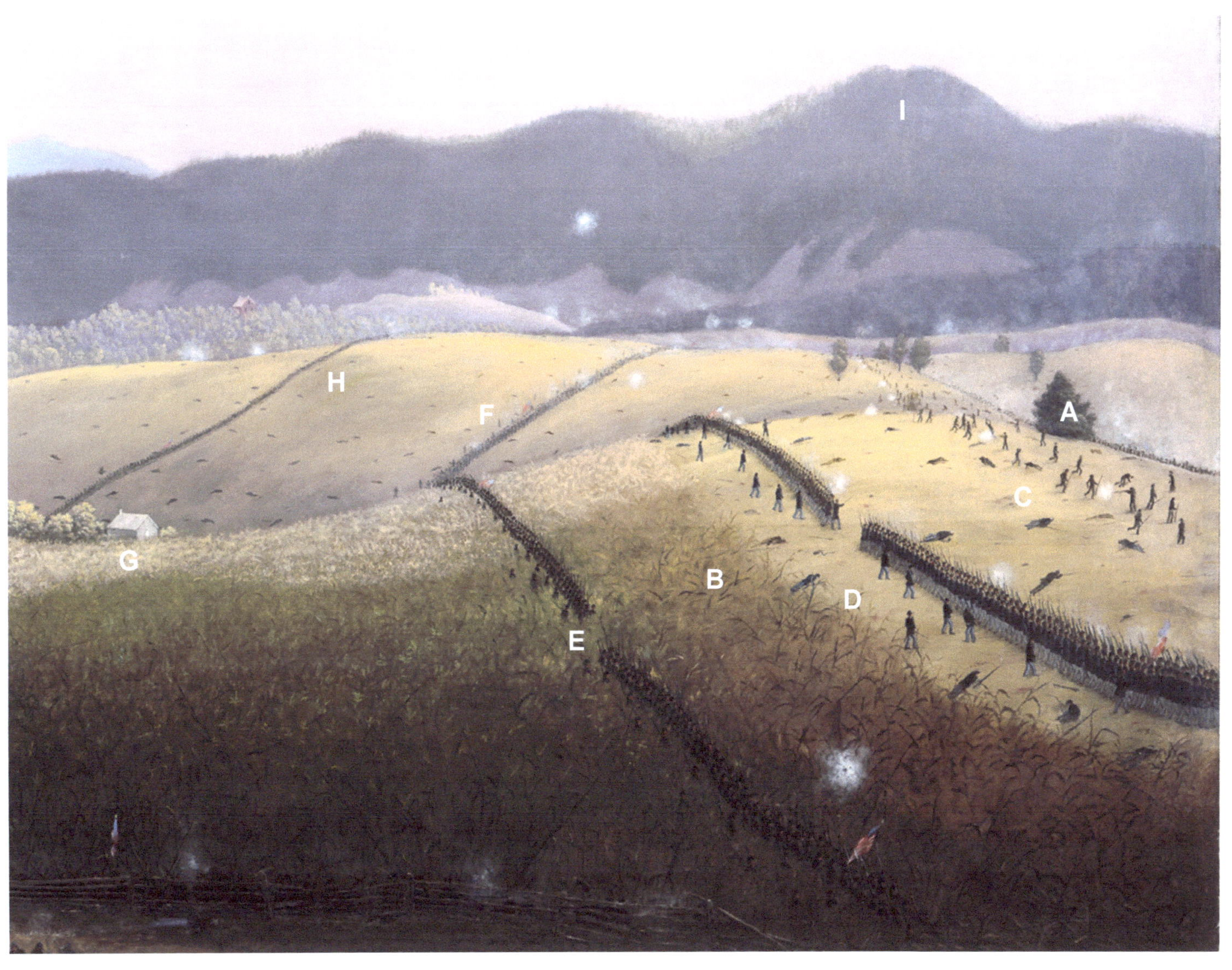

George McClellan planned to launch his initial attack on Lee's left flank, resulting in bloody fighting in the East Woods, West Woods and the Miller Cornfield. Then at 10:00 a.m., he launched his secondary attack against Lee's right flank south of Sharpsburg. However, unlike the I, II and XII Corps who crossed at the undefended Upper Bridge and fords near it, Maj. Gen. Ambrose Burnside's IX Corps was first forced to drive across the Lower Bridge, which was defended by 400-500 Georgia troops. It took three attacks against the bridge and a flanking movement at Snavely Ford, but the Union troops finally captured the bridge at about 1:00 p.m. After a couple of additional hours to get the troops across Antietam Creek, it was time for the Final Attack to begin at about 3:15. p.m.

A Crucial Delay Lower/Burnside Bridge

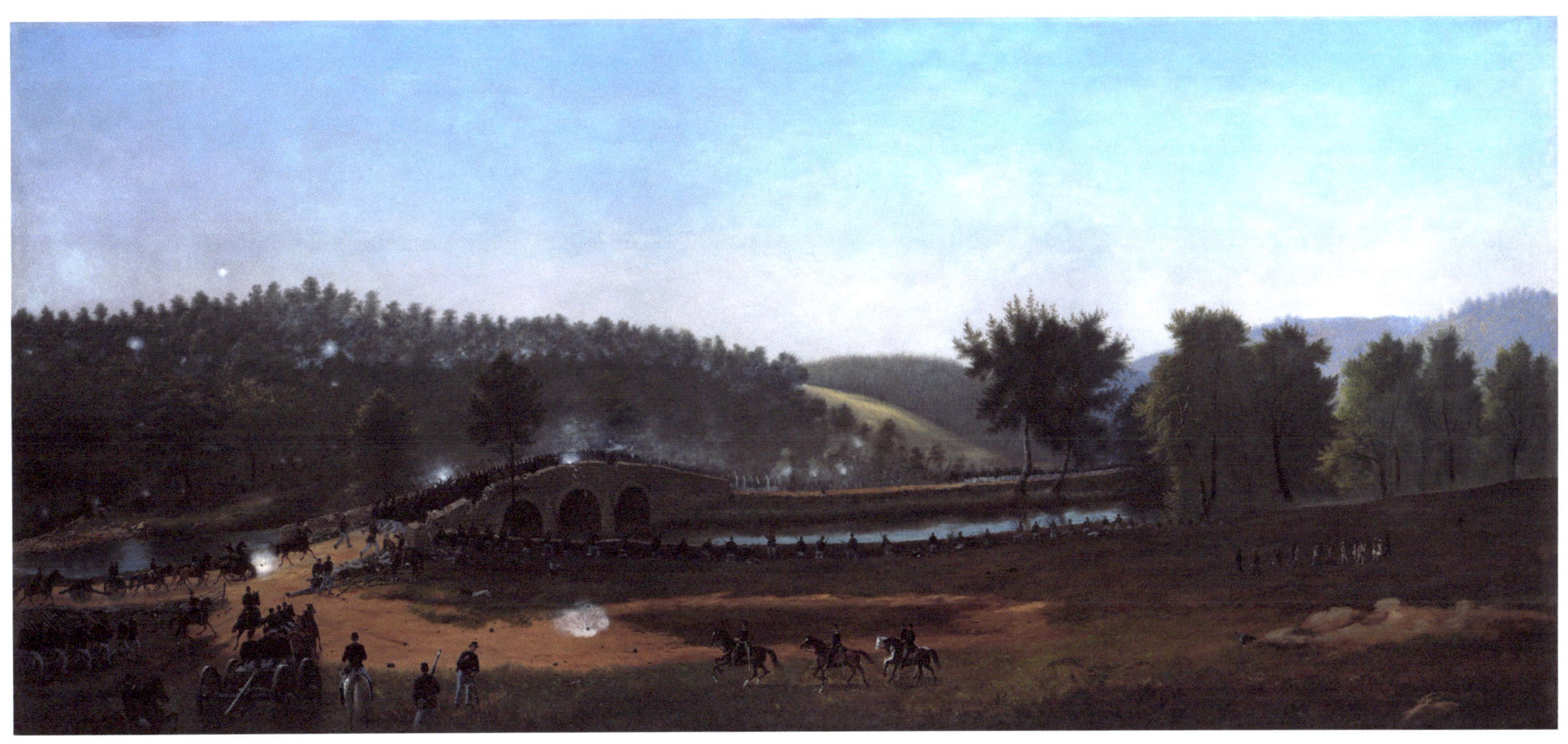

James Hope, *A Crucial Delay,* Oil on Canvas
Courtesy of NPS/Antietam National Battlefield

A. Lower or Burnside Bridge: The 125 by 12 foot long bridge proved to be a barrier for troops attempting to cross it under fire. Confederate artillery fire pounded the Union troops and the bridge, causing damage to both. The shell damage can be easily seen in this section of the painting (and the next).

B. Union troops crossing over the bridge: Once on the bridge, the troops moved rapidly across Antietam Creek.

C. Union troops approaching the bridge: The bottleneck created a traffic jam, but the troops moved forward over the bridge as soon as it cleared. These troops, probably a regiment led by its commanding officer on a horse, are shown approaching the bridge.

D. Union killed and wounded attempting to capture the bridge: The IX Corps sustained about 500 casualties during its three-hour fight to capture the Lower Bridge. These two soldiers are shown pulling a fallen comrade to a gathering site for those needing burials after the battle, usually in long, shallow trenches.

E. Union soldiers firing at the enemy: The Confederate defenders had already retreated by the time the IX Corps was crossing en mass. The skirmish line represented here may have been deployed earlier, after the 51st New York and 51st Pennsylvania had stormed across the bridge at 1:00 p.m., and may be trying to drive the last defenders from the hill overlooking the bridge. However, by the time most of the IX Corps' infantry were crossing, all of the enemy infantry had already retreated.

F. Union cannoneers riding on limber: Two cannon, hooked to limbers, can be seen approaching the bridge. The painting shows cannoneers riding on the limber. This wore out the horses and was dangerous, as the jolting caused by ruts in the road could knock them off their perch, causing injury. This caused most battery officers to discourage the activity.

G. Confederate artillery fire: The Confederate artillery on the distant high ground continued firing on the bridge as Union troops crossed. One shell is shown exploding near a battery's officer, wounding or killing him.

H. Witness tree: This sycamore tree witnessed the fighting for the Lower/Burnside Bridge. It is one of several that remain on the battlefield to this day.

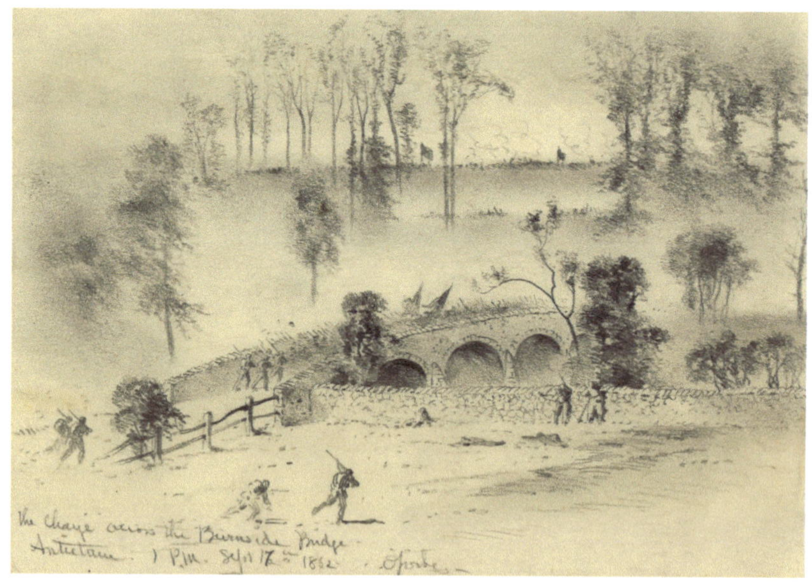

Union attack on the Burnside Bridge by Edwin Forbes
(Library of Congress)

Crucial Delay (Burnside Bridge) Left Side of Painting

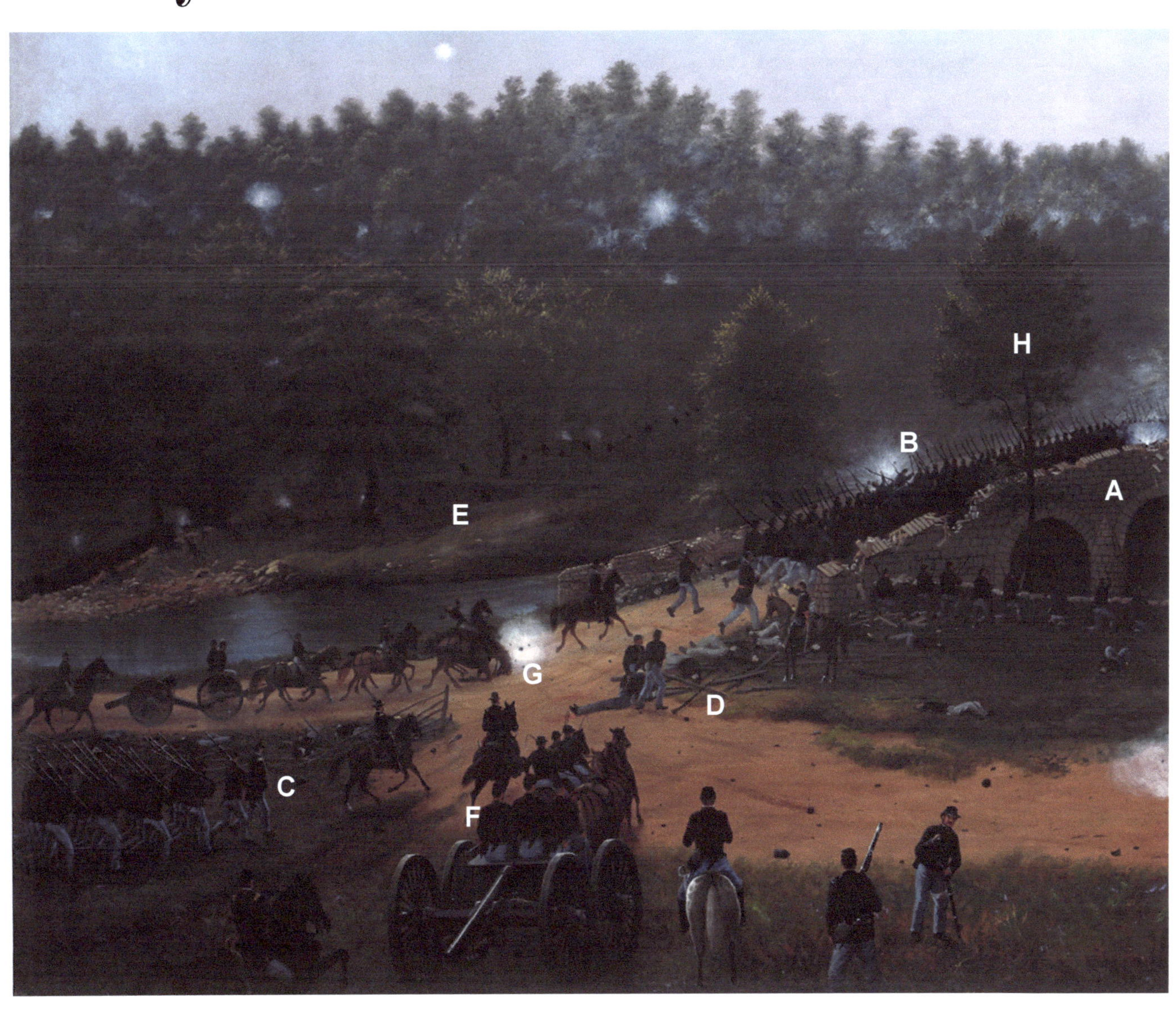

A. Confederate positions overlooking Lower Bridge: Two Confederate regiments, the 2nd and 20th Georgia, numbering less than 500 men were tasked with keeping the 14,000-man IX Corps at bay on the opposite side of Antietam Creek. Although a daunting task, their position on a bluff overlooking the Lower Bridge gave them a distinct advantage, and they were able to repel two Union attempts to take the bridge. The third attempt succeeded because Union troops under Brig. Gen. Isaac Rodman crossed the creek downstream at Snavely Ford and threatened to flank the Georgians. The defenders were also running out of ammunition and men after fighting for almost three hours.

B. Barriers to getting into position to attack: Crossing Antietam Creek was only the first hurdle in getting into position to attack Lee's right flank. The steep bluffs made scaling difficult, especially for the artillery.

C. Union troops marching parallel to Antietam Creek: The steep bluffs overlooking Antietam Creek forced the Union soldiers who had crossed the bridge, to march along what is now called Burnside Bridge Road and then to head west to climb the ridge in less steep areas.

D. Confederate artillery fire: Although the IX Corps had captured the Lower Bridge and driven away the Georgia infantry, Confederate artillery continued pounding the bridge and adjacent areas. The top of the bridge was lined with short wooden slats and several of them can be seen falling into the creek as a Confederate shell explodes nearby. These blasts can be seen in this and the left section of the painting.

E. Union soldiers behind stone wall: During the third and final attack on the Lower Bridge, the 51st Pennsylvania drove down a hill facing Antietam Creek and tried to bully its way across. Intense Confederate fire caused the Pennsylvanians to take refuge behind a stone wall lining Antietam Creek. The men represented here are probably not from the 51st Pennsylvania as that unit had already crossed the bridge. These men are, however, not under fire, as the man loading his rifle in the foreground would not be standing if they were.

F. General Burnside and his staff: The officer leading this small group is Maj. Gen. Ambrose Burnside. Riding behind him is probably Brig. Gen. Jacob Cox. According to Cox, considerable confusion occurred when Burnside, who had been a wing commander during the approach to the battlefield, refused to relinquish that command and reassume Corps command, so Cox continued to oversee the IX Corps. The two officers spent the time at Antietam near each other and when orders arrived, Burnside usually received them, scanned their contents and then handed them to Cox.

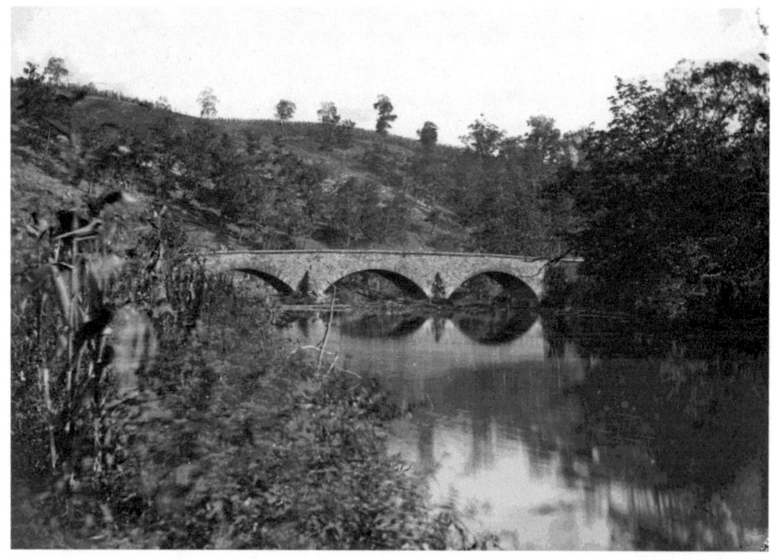

Burnside Bridge
(Library of Congress)

Crucial Delay (Burnside Bridge) Middle of Painting

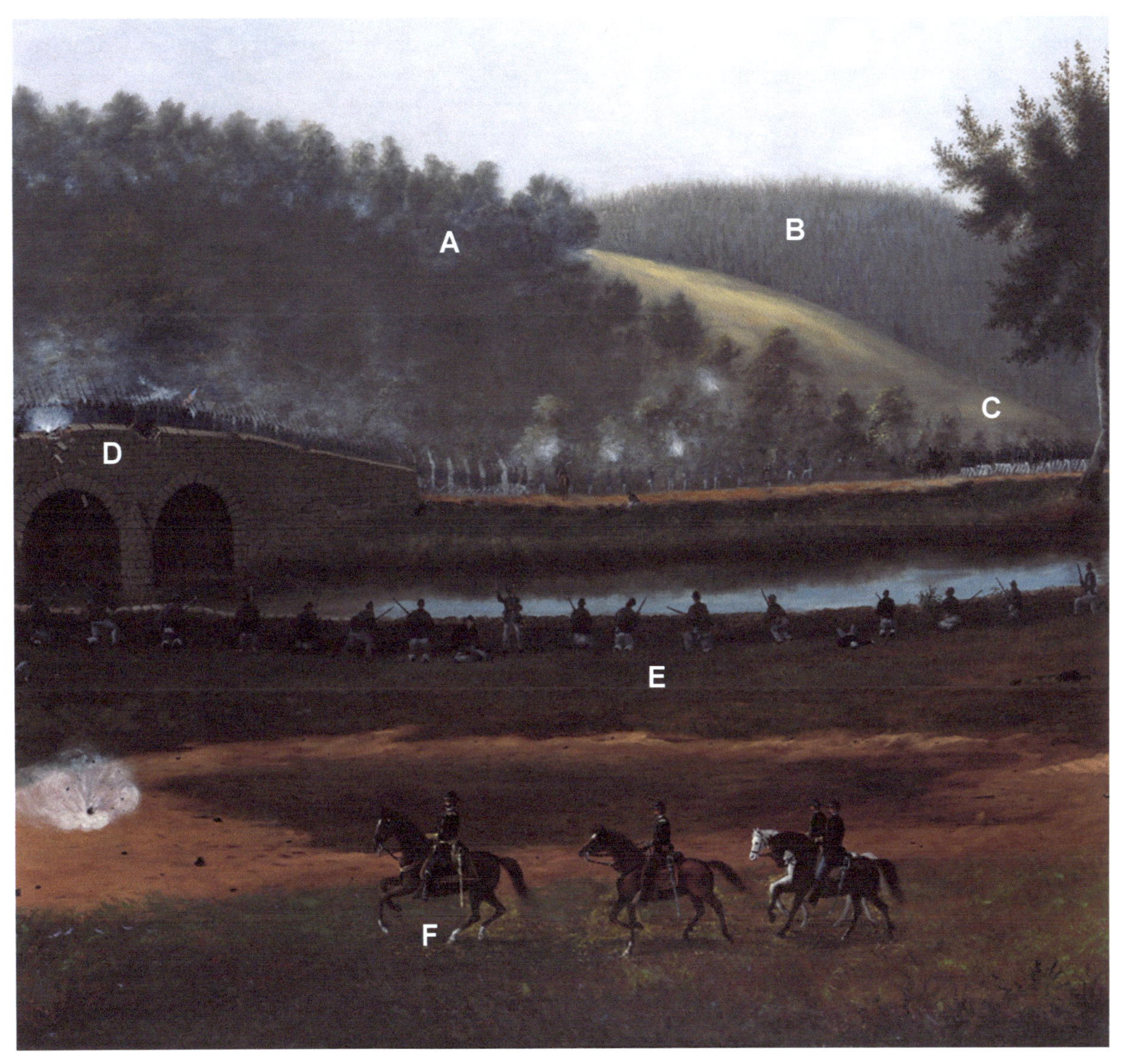

A. March of Union soldiers: The long line of Union soldiers continued making their way toward their final attack positions on Lee's army's right flank.

B. Antietam Creek: The creek was named by local Native American tribes for "swiftly flowing waters." Although not excessively deep, troops could ford the creek only at places where the banks were not steep and the underwater substrate was solid, lest a soldier fall into the water, ruining his ammunition and essentially removing him as an effective fighter.

C. Confederate prisoners being led away: These Confederate soldiers were probably defending the bridge, but it is doubtful there were many, as most of the retreating Georgians simply turned and headed for the rear while the Union troops were still far below the bluff.

D. Terrain: Like so many areas of the battlefield, the terrain was fairly open with relatively few trees. An exception was along the creek bank. A large rock formation, common in the area, can be seen in the foreground. The trees illustrate the importance of the Hudson River School of Art in Hope's paintings.

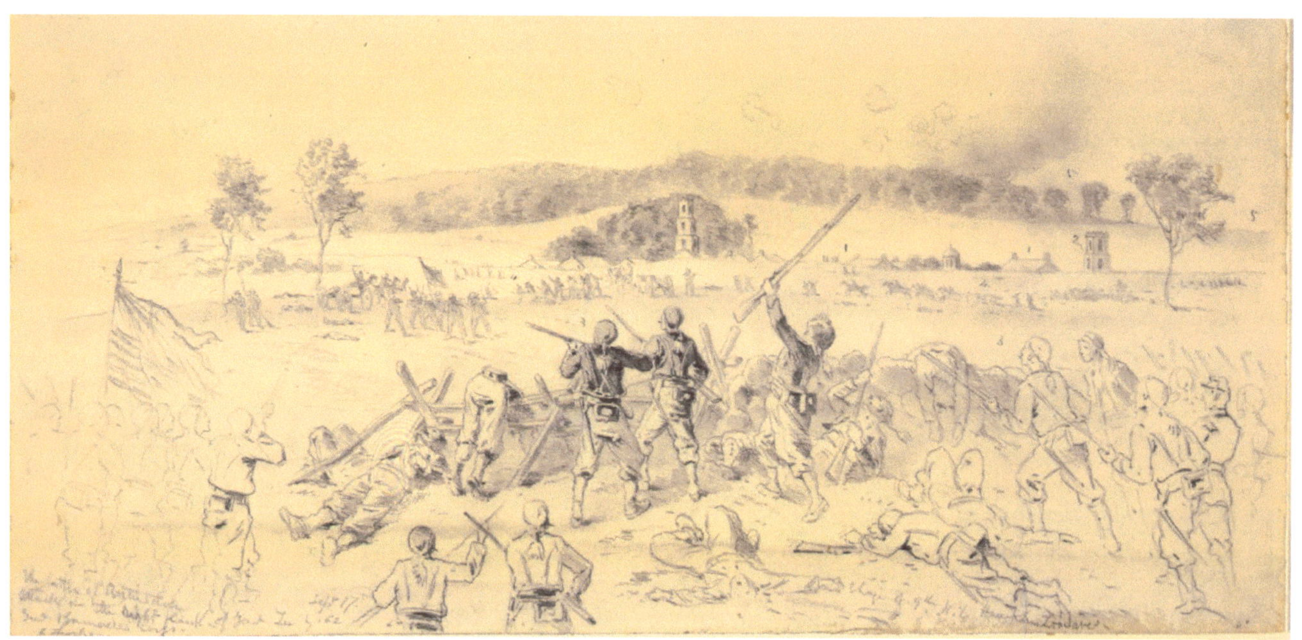

Edwin Forbes' drawing of the Final Attack on the Confederate right flank that occurred after the Burnside Bridge was captured
(Library of Congress)

Crucial Delay (Burnside Bridge) Right Side of Painting

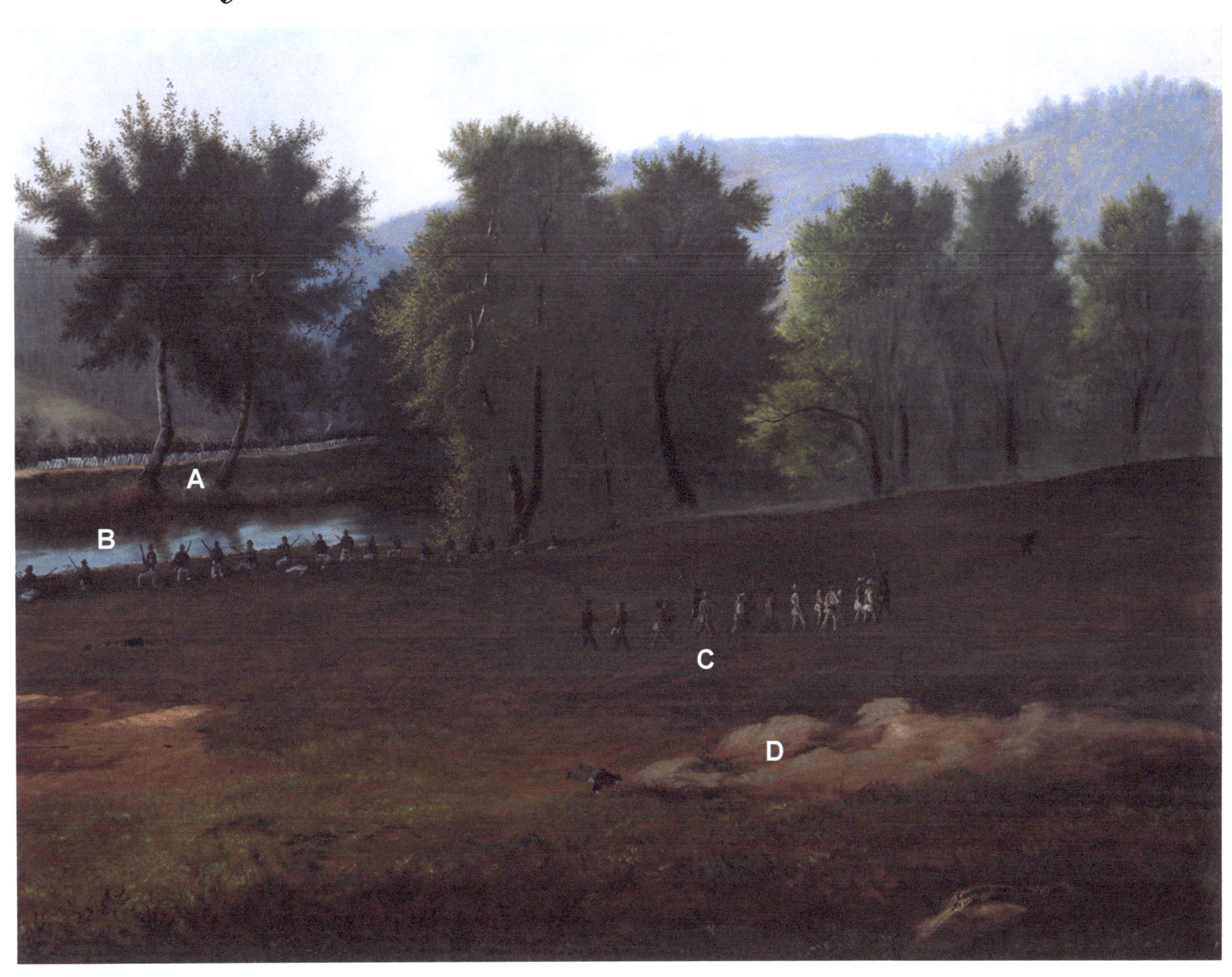

The Wasted Gallantry panorama was the only one of the five featuring an isolated incident involving one Union regiment and several Confederate units. Around 4:30 p.m., Col. William Irwin, commanding the 3rd brigade of Maj. Gen. William Smith's division (VI Corps), ordered the 7th Maine on what can be considered a suicide mission. Irwin was concerned about Confederate snipers in the Piper orchard and farm fields and ordered the regiment to "drive them [the enemy] from those trees and buildings." The order astounded the regiment's commander, Maj. Thomas Hyde, who could see masses of enemy soldiers milling around the Piper property. Hyde asked Irwin to repeat the orders and precisely point out the area he was concerned about. Irwin repeated the orders several times, so Hyde felt duty bound to obey them. Hyde aimed his men toward the Piper farm buildings, traversed the Bloody Lane, and entered the Piper farm fields. Some Union artillery shells accidentally fell among the men, hitting four of them. Masses of Confederate troops fired into the beleaguered unit from several directions and Hyde realized it was time to head back to his lines. The men were forced to halt several times to fire into enemy soldiers who were approaching them from three sides. Hyde's horse was hit, causing the regimental commander to run to catch up with his men after extracting himself. The regiment finally reached safety, but of the 181 men who entered the Piper farm fields 88 became casualties. Hyde would earn the Medal of Honor for his actions that bloody day.

Wasted Gallantry Piper Farm

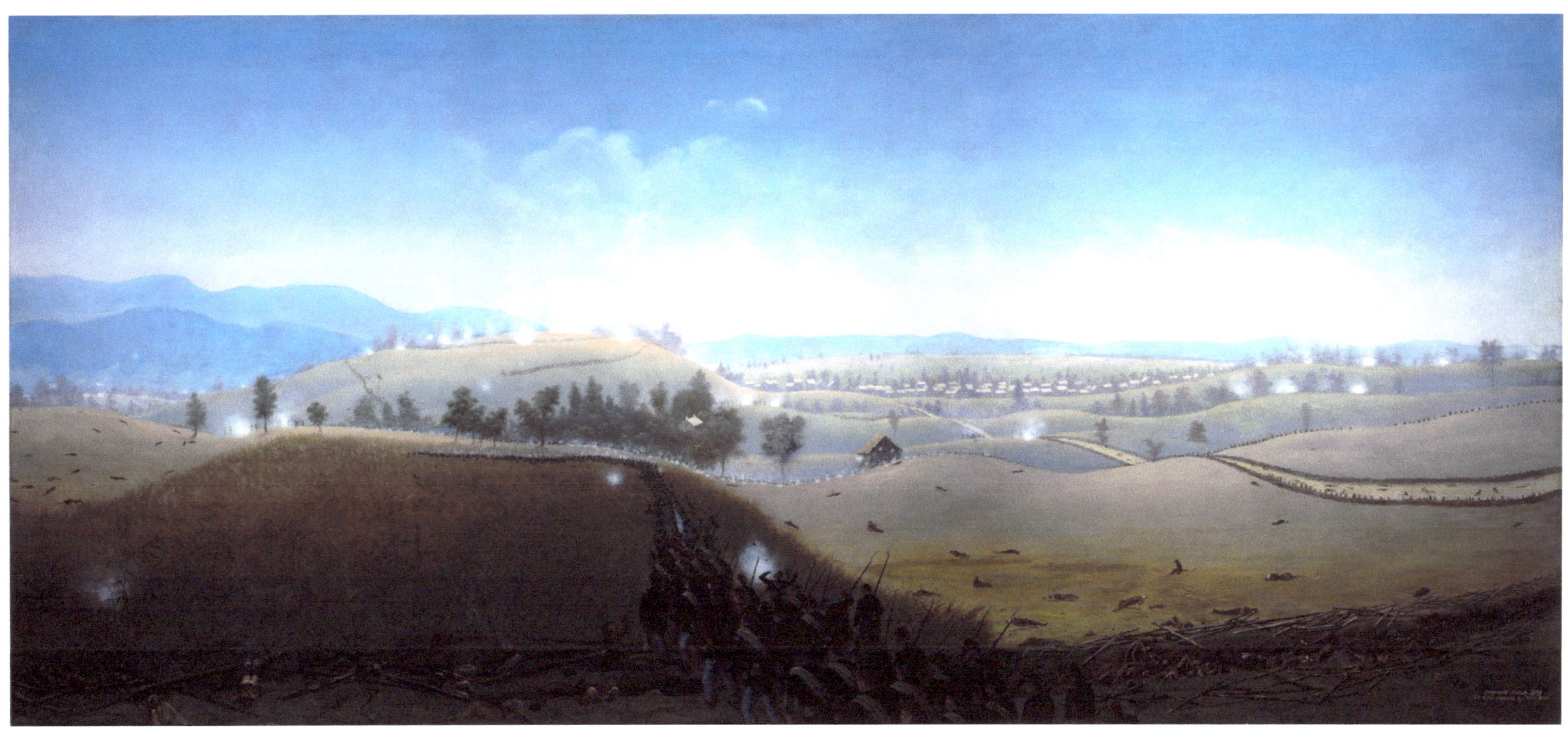

James Hope, *Wasted Gallantry,* Oil on Canvas
Courtesy of (NPS/Antietam National Battlefield)

A. Dead from earlier action in the Piper farm fields: The casualties in the Piper fields resulted from the desperate fighting after the II Corps captured the Sunken Road. The Union goal was never to merely capture the Bloody Lane; it was to head south into the town of Sharpsburg where a wedge would be driven between the two wings of Lee's army and close the enemy's escape route to the Shepherdstown Ford. Fighting occurred in these fields from noon to 1:00 p.m. when the men were told to return beyond the Sunken Road to be resupplied with ammunition, given food, and await the arrival of Brig. Gen. Winfield Hancock who was taking over command of the division from the wounded Gen. Israel Richardson.

B. Piper cornfield: This extensive cornfield played a major role in the battle. Earlier, units from Maj. Gen. Richard Anderson's Confederate division traversed it on their way to the Bloody Lane. Later, as can be seen in the middle part of the painting, the 7th Maine used it to travel toward the Piper house.

C. Head of Hyde's column in the cornfield: According to Maj. Hyde of the 7th Maine, he was initially aiming his column for the left of the Piper house when he became aware of overwhelming Confederate troops descending upon his column.

D. Cemetery Hill: Cemetery Hill dominates the landscape in this part of the panorama and in the center portion. Gen. Lee spent many hours here watching the action, joined by scores of Confederate cannon, raining death and destruction on Union troops. The blasts from the many Confederate cannon can be seen on the hill.

E. Red Hill: This high point on Elk Ridge housed a Union signal station that sent reports to various commands around the battlefield (see photo below)..

F. South Mountain: The mighty mountain range looms beyond Elk Ridge.

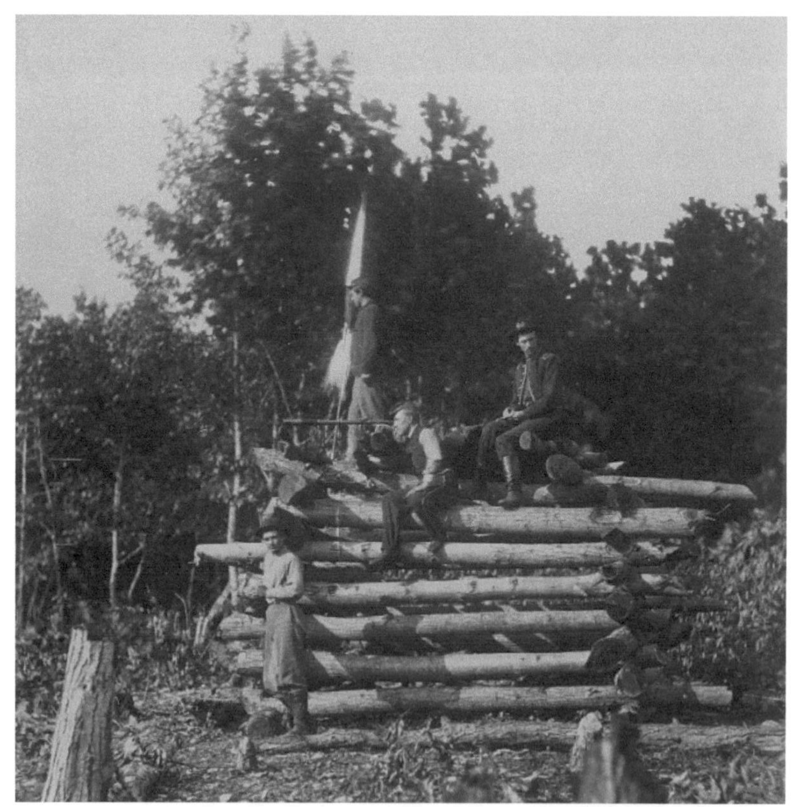

Alexander Gardner photo of Union signal station on Red Hill
(Library of Congress)

Wasted Gallantry (Piper Farm) Left Side of Painting

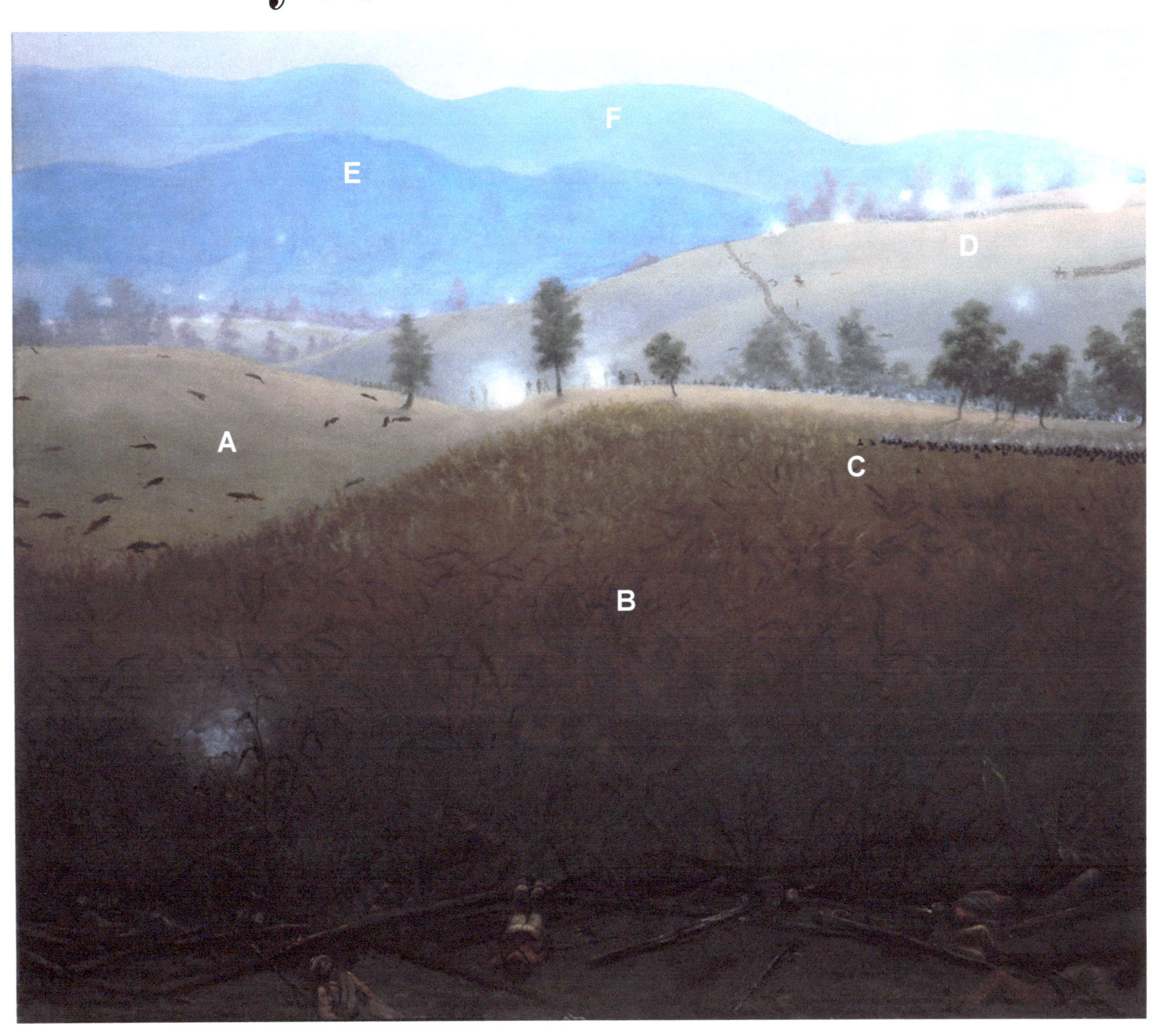

A. Town of Sharpsburg: The small town of Sharpsburg can be seen in the distance. The 1860 census counted a population of around 1,300. The census also listed 150 enslaved persons and 50 slave owners. The town was held by the Confederates during the battle and its main street headed directly to the Potomac River at Shepherdstown, where a ford spanned the river. Although no fighting occurred in the town, many of its buildings sustained shell damage.

B. Piper house: The 184 acre farm was owned by Henry and Elizabeth Piper. It contained the only commercial apple orchard in the region. The Pipers, like most of the residents of Sharpsburg, had left their homes prior to the battle and returned on September 19. They were initially relieved to find the house and barn in fairly good shape, but lying underneath their piano were two dead Confederate soldiers. They also found their personal possessions strewn around the buildings and caught Union soldiers butchering some of their livestock. Mr. Piper filed a claim with the government to cover his losses and was awarded $2,488, but never received payment because he did not produce a certificate of loyalty. The house was used by Confederate Gen. James Longstreet as his headquarters during part of the battle.

C. Piper barn: The large barn could easily be seen from Hagerstown Pike, the Sunken Road, and other areas of the battlefield. It, like other large buildings, would become a hospital after the battle.

D. The 7th Maine marching through the Piper cornfield: The small regiment marched south toward the Piper house on the afternoon of September 17 to drive Confederates from around the Piper farm buildings who were firing at Union batteries near the Sunken Road and Piper orchard. So incredulous was regimental commander, Maj. Thomas Hyde, that he asked his commander, Col. William Irwin, to repeat the orders several times. An exasperated Irwin finally said, "Those are your orders sir." Without recourse, Hyde led his men into the Piper cornfield. Hyde initially aimed his men toward the corner of the Piper barn, but when he was hit by an oblique fire, he angled his men to the left to take advantage of protective terrain there.

E. Artillery fire: Both friendly fire from Union batteries and hostile fire from the Confederates raked the 7th Maine's line as it marched toward the Piper buildings.

F. George T. Anderson's Confederate brigade: These troops were initially hidden from view, but stood and fired into Hyde's men as they approached. Gen. D. H. Hill also led a band of Confederates along the Piper farm lane toward Hyde's flank. With the enemy closing in, Hyde ordered a retreat. Most reached the safety of their lines, but it was a close call.

Wasted Gallantry (Piper Farm) Middle of Painting

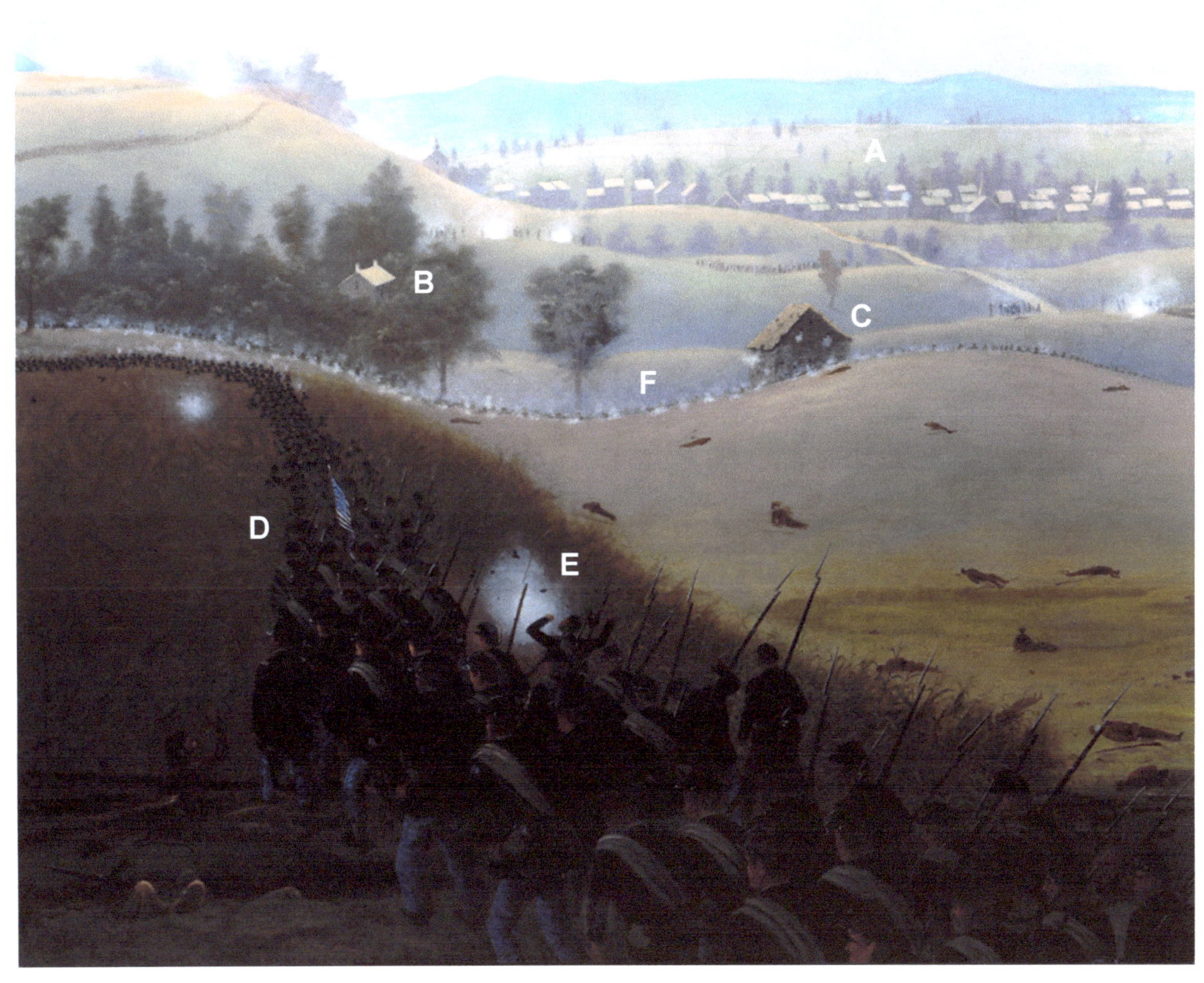

A. Hagerstown Pike: The turnpike ran from Hagerstown to Sharpsburg and was important in moving troops around the battlefield. For example, after 10:00 a.m., Maj. Gen. Richard Anderson's Confederate division arrived in Sharpsburg after an all-night march from Harpers Ferry. It was immediately dispatched to reinforce the besieged Bloody Lane. The 4,000 men used the Hagerstown Pike to reach the contested area; most making a right into the Piper farm fields, reforming, and then heading north toward the Sunken Road.

B. The Confederate living and dead in the Hagerstown Pike: As the men of the 7th Maine made their way toward the Piper buildings, Confederate infantry along the fence opened fire on their right flank. Many of the dead in the road were probably from Gen. Richard Anderson's division who were hit by enemy artillery fire as they made their way toward the Bloody Lane earlier in the day.

C. Reel Ridge: The cannon blasts are from scores of Confederate guns on Reel Ridge, to the right (west) of Hagerstown Pike. These guns were firing into the II and VI Corps troops around and beyond the Sunken Road.

D. Bloody Lane: Barely visible in the other two portions of this panorama, but more obvious here, are the Confederate dead and wounded in the Bloody Lane. Hyde and his men did their best to avoid stepping on any of the wounded. It was a horrible experience that few would ever forget.

E. Dead Confederate soldier: See similarity of this dead soldier to letter G in Aftermath at Bloody Lane, (middle of painting).

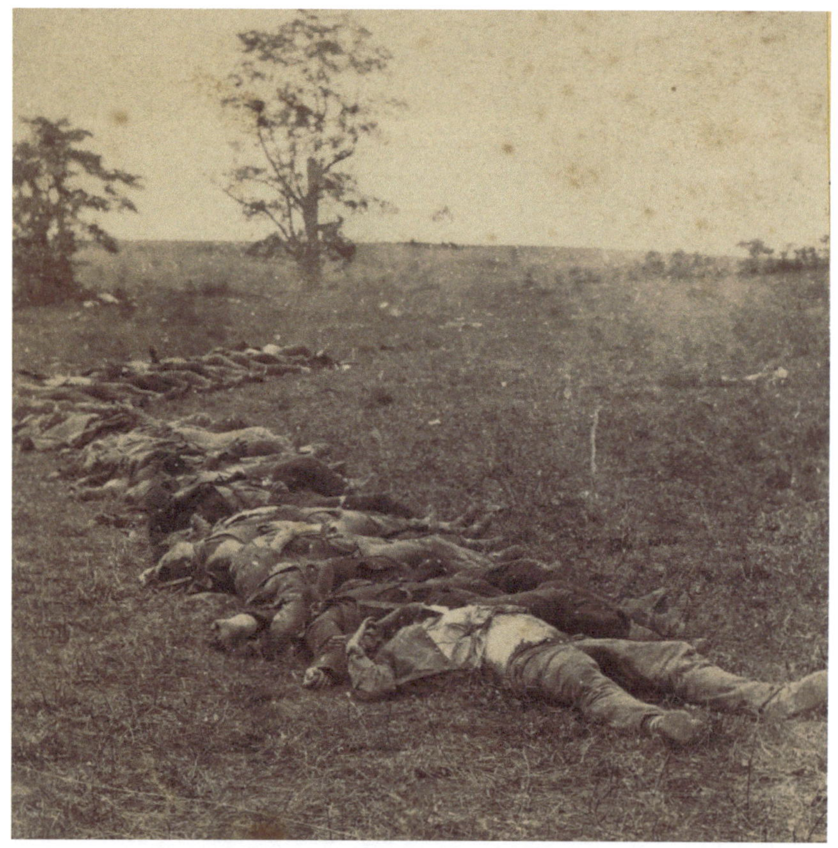

Alexander Gardner photo of dead Confederates prepared for burial.
(Library of Congress)

Wasted Gallantry (Piper Farm) Right Side of Painting

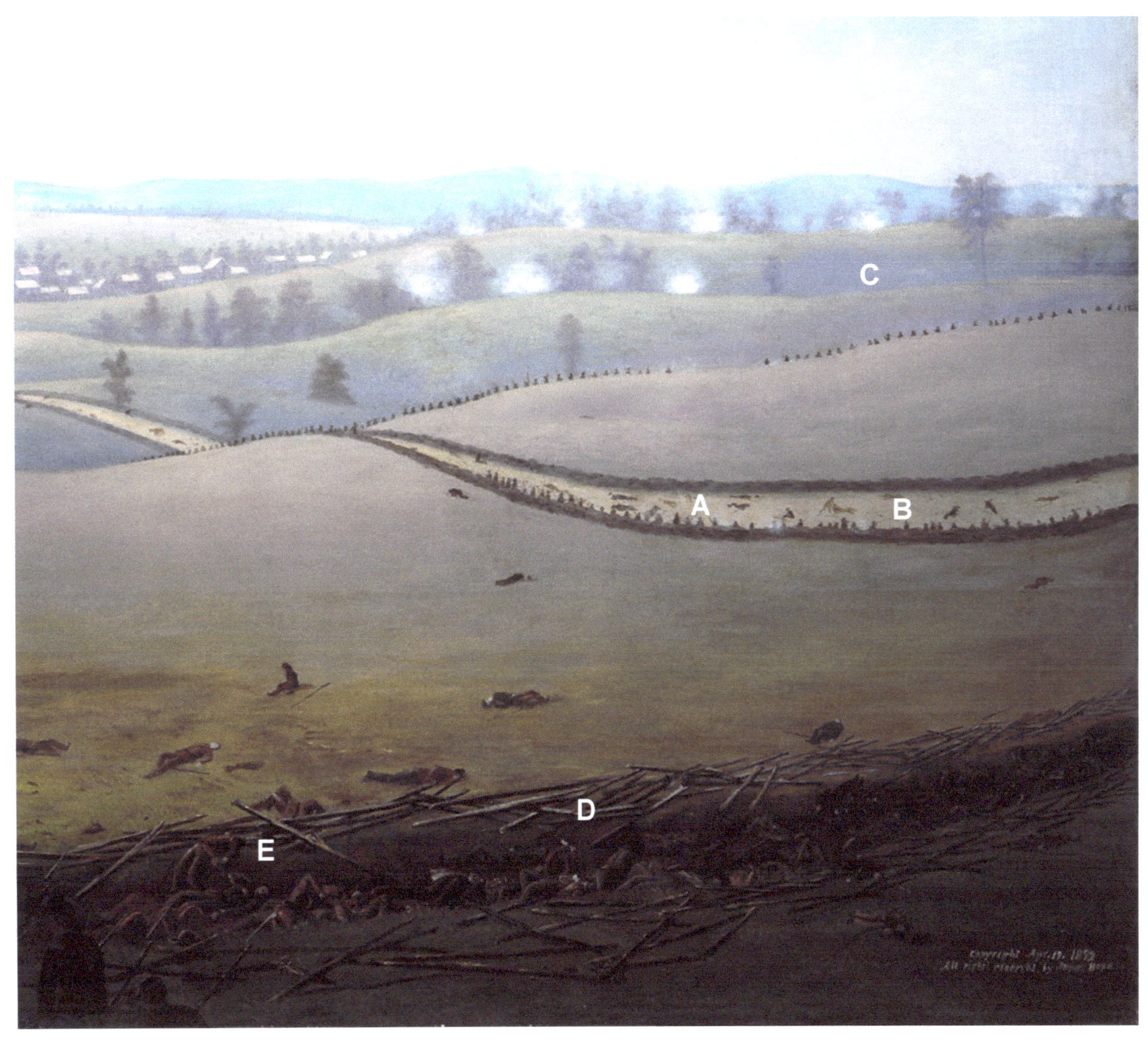

This painting is the only one in the series that covers the aftermath of the bloody affair, and unlike the others, was almost destroyed by the flood that besieged the region during the 1930's. Fortunately, Hope painted a small version of the painting that exists today. It is owned by the U.S. Army.

The Confederate dead in the Bloody Lane, in some cases three to five deep, are depicted in detail in his panorama. Although Hope did not include bloody corpses in his painting, their abundance and grotesque positions convey the sense of horror for those who fought in the battle. The Sunken Road stretched from Hagerstown Pike to Boonsboro Pike, and years of wagons making their way along this path, coupled with erosion, created a perfect defensive position for the Confederates attempting to keep Union troops from capturing the town of Sharpsburg. That part of the Sunken Road directly facing the Union onslaught was renamed the "Bloody Lane." Two Union divisions, numbering over 11,000 men attacked the Confederates under Maj. Gen. D. H. Hill (later reinforced by Gen. Richard Anderson's division) from 9:15 through noon, when the defenders were forced from their defensive positions and into the Piper farm fields between the Sunken Road and Sharpsburg. The painting accurately reflects the curve in the road that separated two of Hill's brigades. Those corpses in the foreground are men from Brig. Gen. Robert Rodes' Alabama brigade; the dead beyond the bend are from Brig. Gen. George B. Anderson's North Carolina brigade.

The Aftermath at Bloody Lane

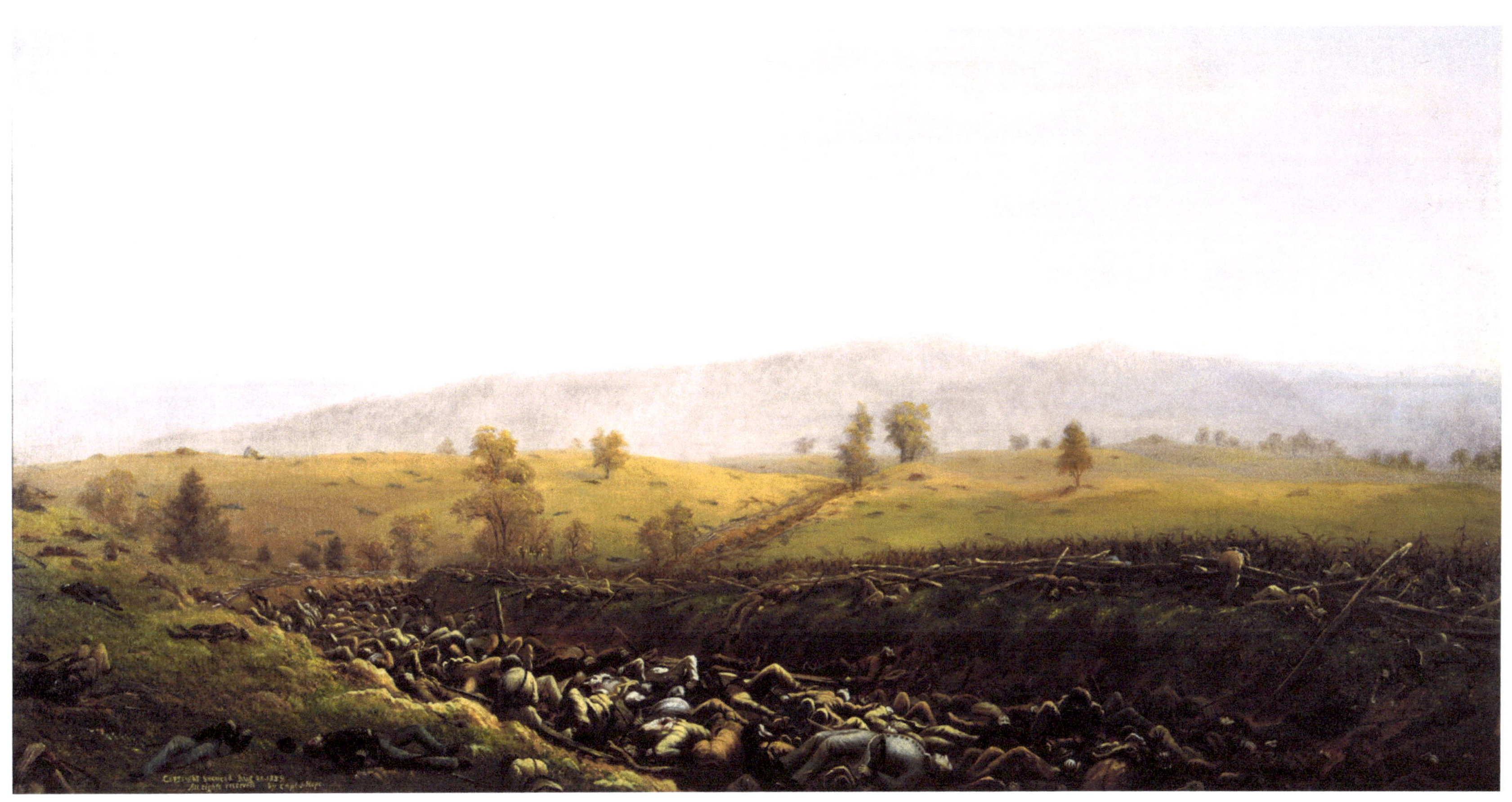

James Hope, *The Aftermath at Bloody Lane,* Oil on Canvas
Courtesy of NPS/Antietam National Battlefield

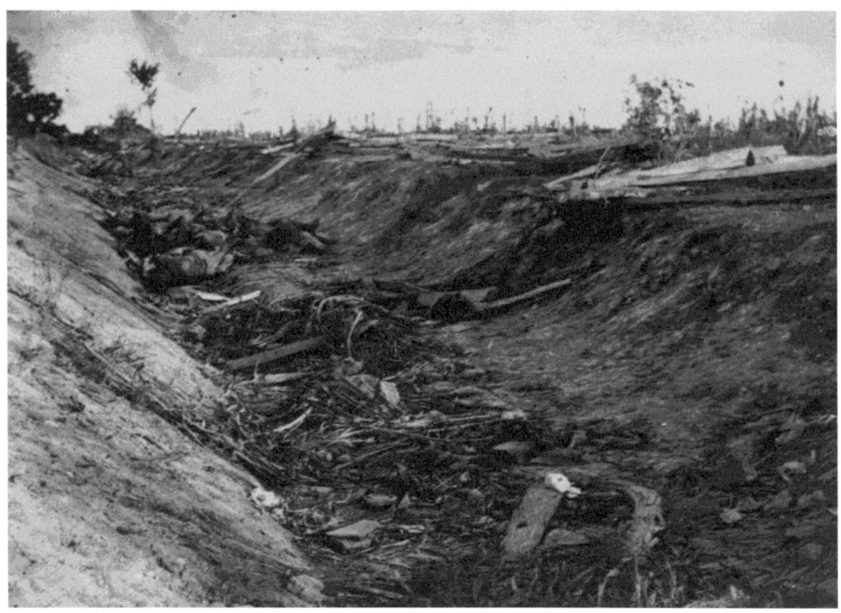

Debris of battle in the Bloody Lane
(Library of Congress)

A. Confederate dead in the Bloody Lane: Most of these dead are from the 6th Alabama Infantry under Col. John Gordon, who was wounded five times in this battle, but lived to command one of Lee's three corps during the retreat to Appomattox Courthouse in 1865. He purportedly told Lee before the fighting: "These men are going to stay here, General, till the sun goes down or victory is won." He was unable to keep his word. The crush of the dead and wounded in the Sunken Road illustrate how difficult it must have been for the unscathed to continue defending the road.

B. Fences: Upon taking position in the Bloody Lane, Gen. Hill ordered the men to pulled down the worm fence on the left side of the road to provide additional protection to the defenders.

C. Dead Union soldiers: One expects to see dead Union soldiers on the left of the painting, as that is the direction of their attack. Many can be seen in the foreground and on the hill in the distance. However, the numbers were actually much greater. As many as 500 Union soldiers were killed near the Bloody Lane. Most of these men in the distance would have been from the venerable Irish Brigade.

D. Confederates outside of the Bloody Lane: The numerous dead Confederates reflect the ill-fated counterattack made by defenders of the Bloody Lane after they had repulsed several Union attacks.

E. Elk Ridge: The northern extension can be seen in front of South Mountain.

F. South Mountain: Is barely visible in the background.

The Aftermath at Bloody Lane Left Side of Painting

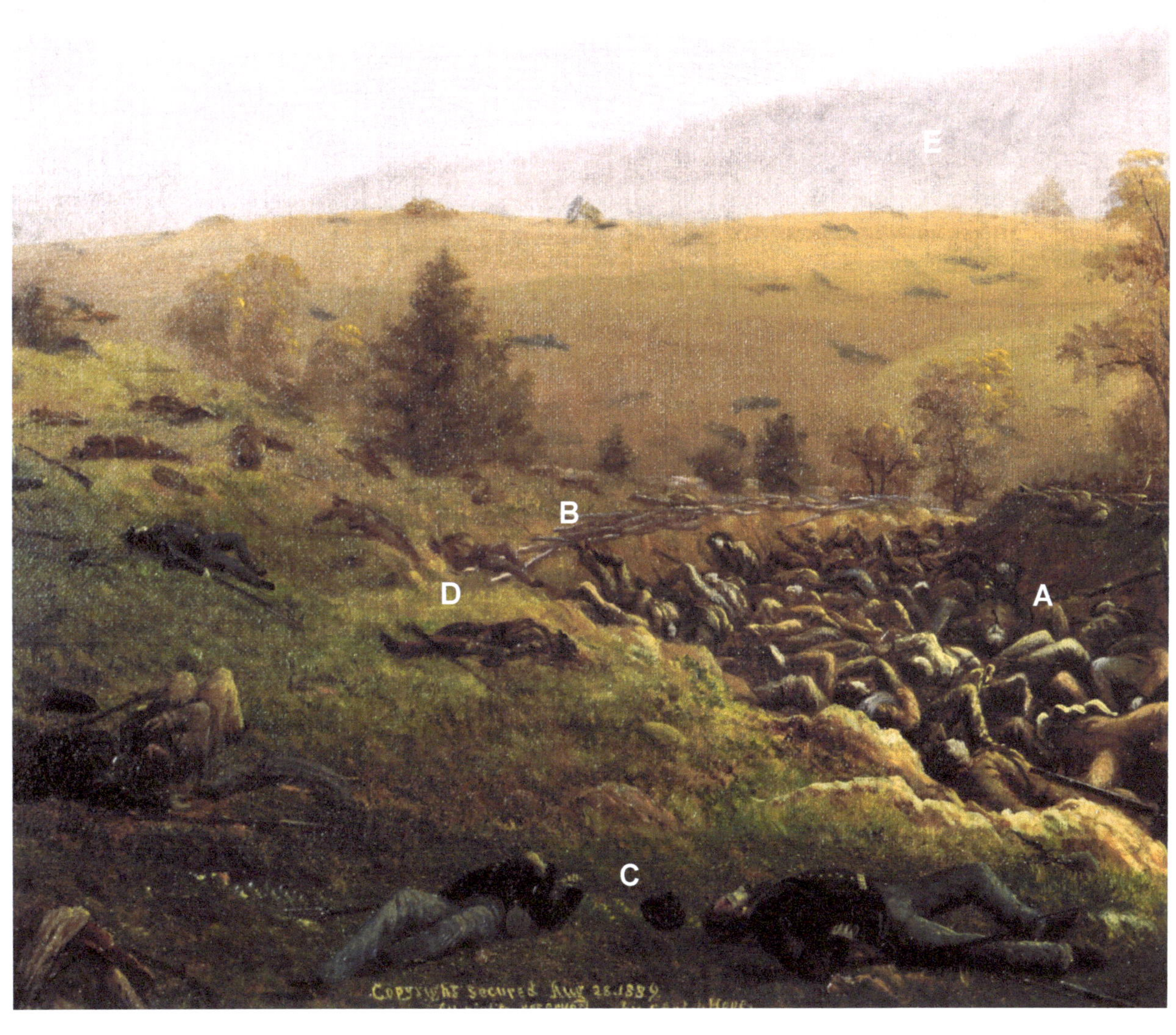

A. Ridgeline: The men of Maj. Gen. Israel Richardson's division attacked over this hill. Although initially protected when behind its brow, they advanced against the Bloody Lane without a shred of protection and were mowed down by the Confederates in the Sunken Road. Richardson launched two of his brigades against the Bloody Lane: first the Irish Brigade and then Brig. Gen. John Caldwell's brigade.

B. Right side of Bloody Lane: Although this part of the Bloody Lane does not appear to house dead Confederates, it actually rivaled the left side of the painting in the numbers of the dead after the battle.

C. Union breakthrough: After the fighting raged for three hours, the combined 61st/64th New York regiments of Caldwell's brigade wrapped around the right and rear of the Bloody Lane, rolling up the Confederate line and finally forcing it to be abandoned.

D. Balanced dead Confederate soldier: Several Union soldiers who survived the battle recalled a dead Confederate, who died instantly after being shot in the head, but remained in a firing position as his body was so perfectly balanced.

E. Dead Confederate officer: Some Union soldiers believe the dead Confederate officer lying atop his men is Lt. Col. James Lightfoot. He assumed command of the 6th Alabama after Col. Gordon fell wounded and was responsible for misinterpreting orders, causing his men to vacate the Bloody Lane prematurely. He would have been killed just as his men were retreating, hence his body is lying atop the others who had been killed earlier.

F. Hope's use of the Gardner photo: Comparing the Alexander Gardner photo (to the right) with this portion of the Hope painting, one can see how the painter used the photo when executing his work. The letter is on the bottom (middle) of the Gardner photo.

G: Dead Confederate soldier comparison: Hope apparently used similar images in his five panoramas. See E on Wasted Gallantry (right side of painting) for a comparison.

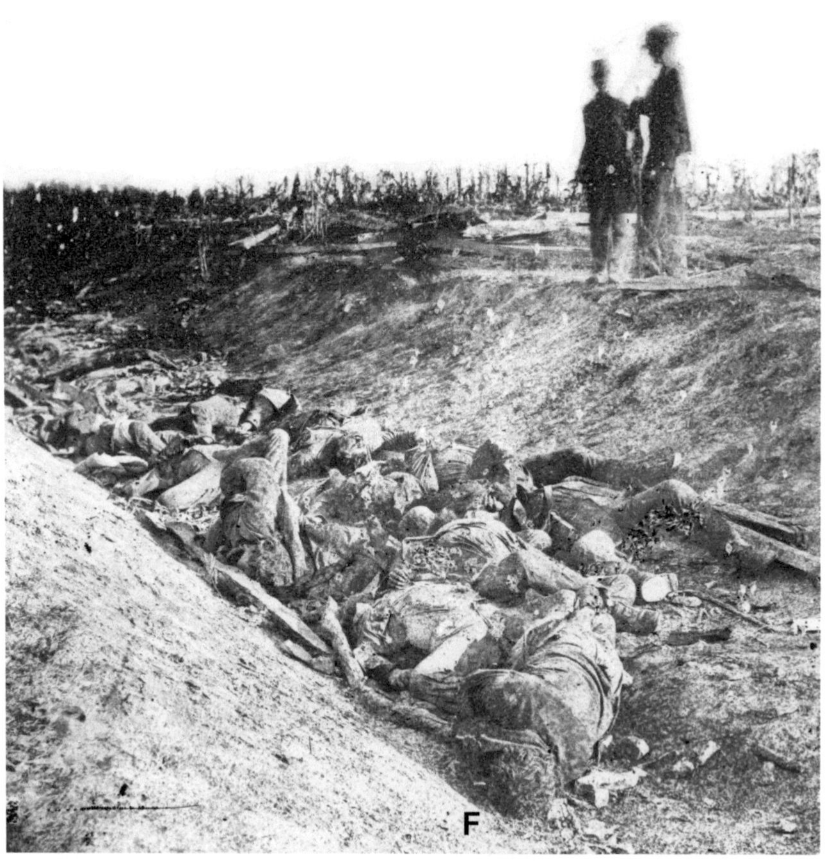

Confederate dead in the Bloody Lane
(Library of Congress)

The Aftermath at Bloody Lane Center of Painting

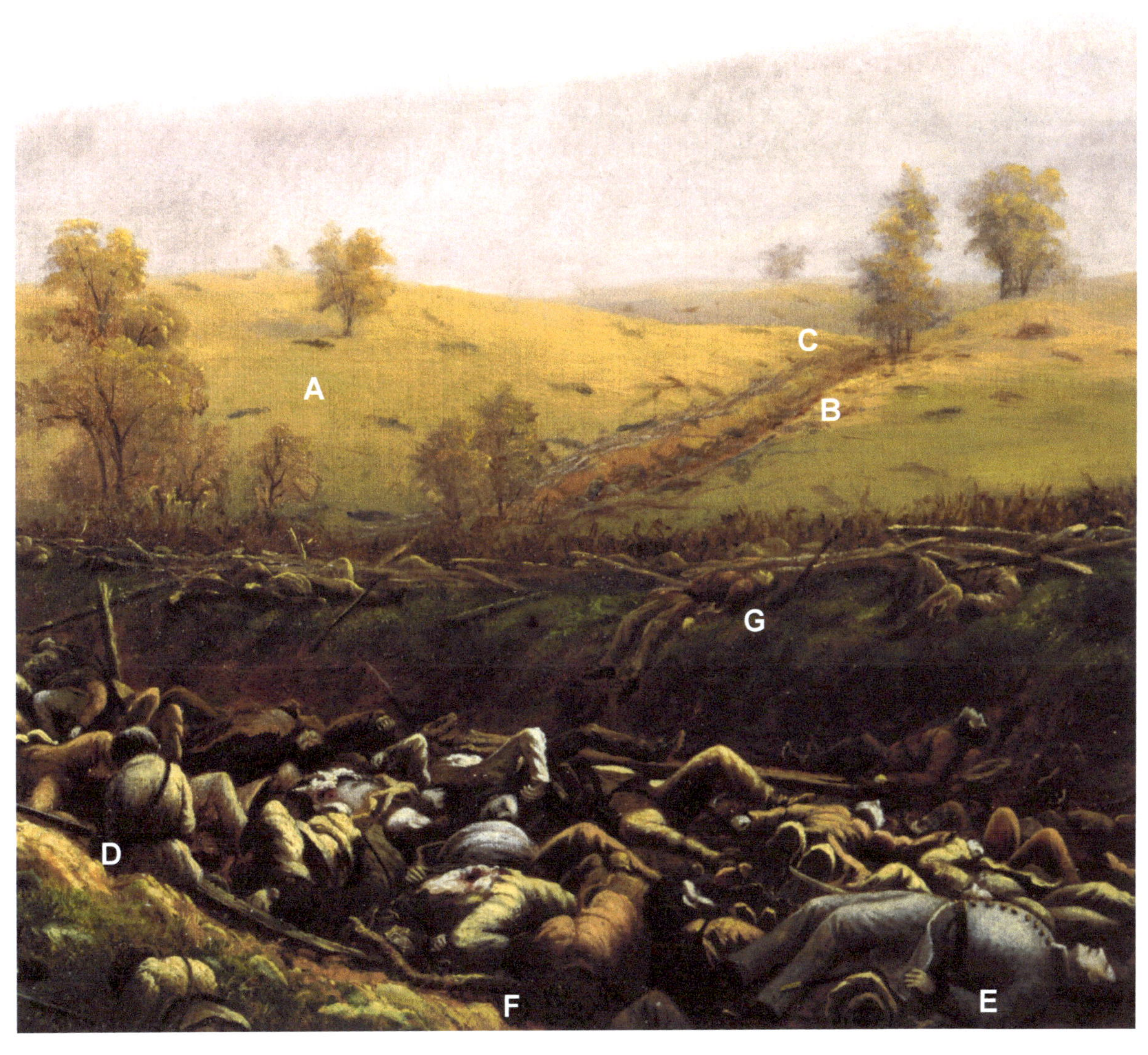

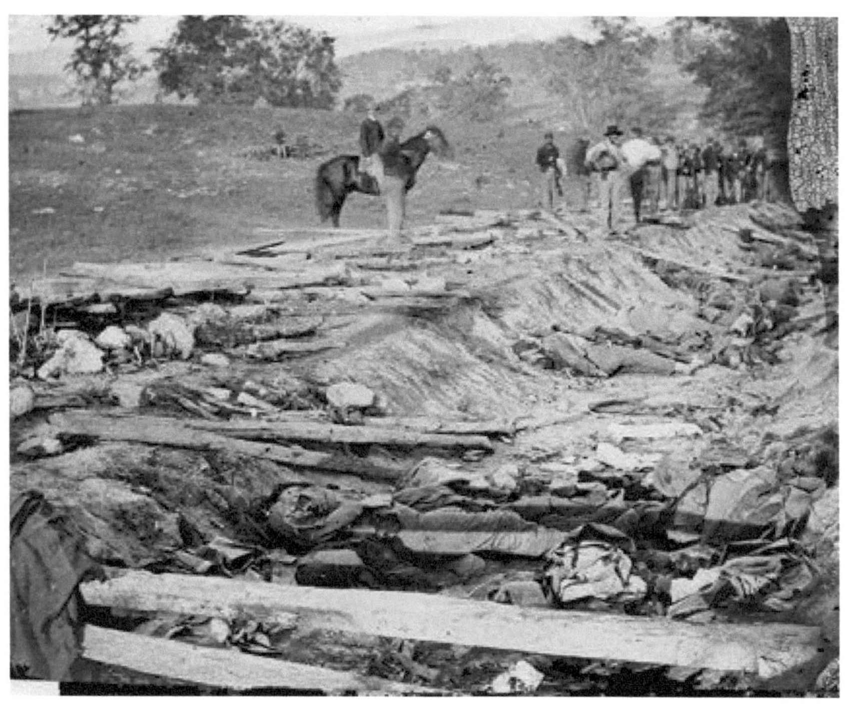

Soldiers examining Confederate dead in the Bloody Lane
(Library of Congress)

A. Dead Confederate lying on fence: Many Union soldiers recalled a dead Confederate soldier lying on a fence after being shot eight times during the battle.

B. Dead Confederate soldiers: These dead Confederate soldiers show the variety of "uniforms" they wore—some gray, others varying shades of butternut. One of the dead soldiers has his blanket looped around his shoulder—a common occurrence in the Confederate army. Like the sitting soldier in the middle part of the canvas, this section also contains a body which did not fall.

C. Piper farm fields: After the fall of the Bloody Lane, the fight shifted to the Piper farm fields, where the Confederate soldiers desperately attempted to keep the victorious Union troops from attacking Sharpsburg. If successful, the Union troops could have cleaved Lee's army in half and cut off his escape route to the Potomac River. Depletion of ammunition, exhaustion, and the mortal wounding of Maj. Gen. Richardson caused the fighting to end at 1:00 p.m. without gaining the vital town.

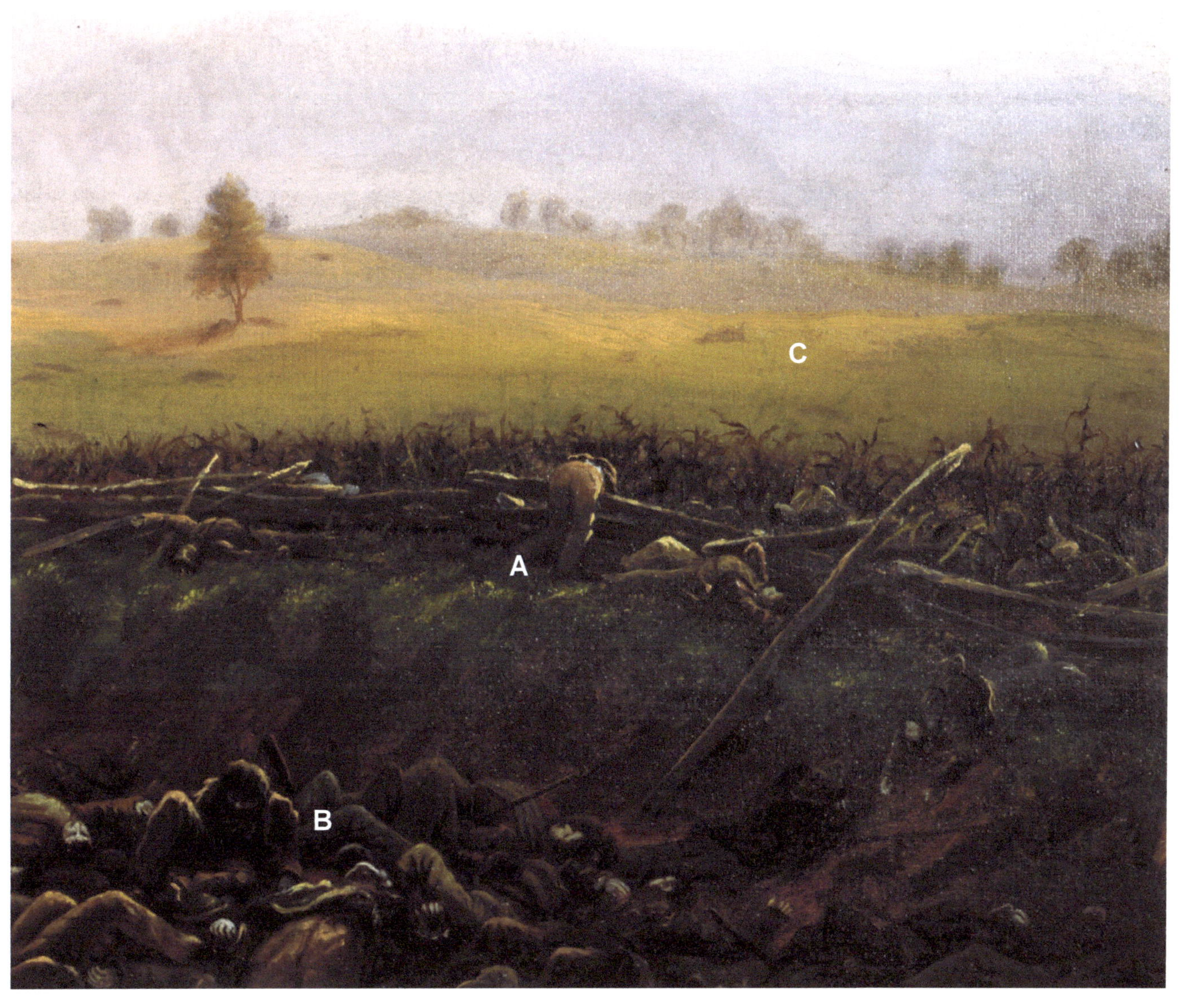

The Aftermath at Bloody Lane
Right Side of Painting

HOPE'S GLEN ART GALLERY.

Now on exhibition, at Hope's Glen Art Gallery, Watkins Glen, N. Y., a superb collection of

OVER ONE HUNDRED OIL PAINTINGS,
AND SKETCHES,

By J. HOPE, LATE OF 82 FIFTH AVENUE, N. Y.,

From various parts of this country and Europe, among which are the prominent scenes in Watkins Glen, his celebrated

RAINBOW FALLS,

his great Historical Painting of the

ARMY OF THE POTOMAC,

at Cumberland Landing, valued at Twenty-five Thousand Dollars,

Also GEM OF THE FOREST, FOREST GLEN, SYLVAN DELL, SCENE IN NORWAY, SCENE ON THE RHINE, &c., &c.

New ones are being constantly added.   Read the Opinions of the Press.

Advertisement for Hope's Glen Art Gallery
Courtesy of the NPS/Antietam National Battlefield

Sources

Freeman, Larry, *The Hope Paintings*. Watkins Glen, NY: Century House, 1961.

Gottfried, Bradley M. *Brigades of Antietam*. Sharpsburg, MD: The Antietam Institute, 2021.

"The Famous Hope Canvases," by the Fifth Avenue Art Galleries (1904)

United States War Department. *The War of the Rebellion: A Compilation of the Official Records of the Union and Confederate Armies*. 128 volumes. Washington, U.S. Government Printing Office, 1880-1901.

"Witness to Battle: The story of September 17, 1862, as told through the paintings of Captain James Hope." Western Maryland Interpretive Association.

https://wizzley.com/james-hope-in-watkins-glen-civil-war-artist/

Acknowledgements

This book is made possible with the assistance of several individuals. Keith Snyder, Chief Ranger at the Antietam National Military Park graciously provided many files of the Hope Antietam paintings and allowed use of other images. Brian Baracz patiently answered a myriad of questions about the paintings and the events they portray. He also read the manuscript and made several substantive suggestions. Laura and Ed Marfut did a wonderful job reviewing the manuscript and their comments were incorporated into the final product. Thanks also to James Rosebrock for providing insights on the artillery sections of the booklet.